The Literature of Cinema

ADVISORY EDITOR: **MARTIN S. DWORKIN**
INSTITUTE OF PHILOSOPHY AND POLITICS OF EDUCATION
TEACHER'S COLLEGE, COLUMBIA UNIVERSITY

THE LITERATURE OF CINEMA presents a comprehensive selection from the multitude of writings about cinema, rediscovering materials on its origins, history, theoretical principles and techniques, aesthetics, economics, and effects on societies and individuals. Included are works of inherent, lasting merit and others of primarily historical significance. These provide essential resources for serious study and critical enjoyment of the "magic shadows" that became one of the decisive cultural forces of modern times.

THE
ITALIAN CINEMA

By

VERNON JARRATT

ARNO PRESS & THE NEW YORK TIMES
NEW YORK • 1972

Reprint Edition 1972 by Arno Press Inc.

Reprinted from a copy in the Library of John P. Lowe
LC# 78-169338
ISBN 0-405-03898-4

The Literature of Cinema - Series II
ISBN for complete set: 0-405-03887-9
See last pages of this volume for titles.

Manufactured in the United States of America

THE ITALIAN CINEMA

THE
ITALIAN CINEMA

By

VERNON JARRATT

THE FALCON PRESS

First published in 1951
by The Falcon Press
6 & 7 Crown Passage, Pall Mall,
London, S.W 1
Printed in Great Britain
by
Northern Publishing Co. Ltd.
Copyright 1951
by Vernon Jarratt

CONTENTS

Editor's Preface   page VII

Author's Foreword   IX

CHAPTER

1. EARLY DAYS   11

2. THE ARRIVAL OF THE STAR SYSTEM AND PRODUCTION DURING
   THE FIRST WORLD WAR   20

3. THE YEARS AFTER THE FIRST WORLD WAR   28

4. THE COMING OF SOUND AND THE FASCIST PERMEATION OF
   THE CINEMA   35

5. THE YEARS BEFORE AND DURING THE SECOND WORLD WAR   44

6. THE POST-WAR RENAISSANCE—PART 1   57

7. THE POST-WAR RENAISSANCE—PART 2   73

8. A NOTE ON DOCUMENTARY   89

9. SOME NOTES ON ITALIAN DIRECTORS AND ITALIAN PRODUC-
   TION METHODS   94

APPENDICES

1. A LIST OF ITALIAN FILMS DIRECTED FROM 1930–1946 BY THE
   LEADING DIRECTORS   101

2. CAST AND CREDIT LISTS OF THE MORE IMPORTANT POST-
   WAR FILMS   103

INDICES

1. FILM TITLES   109

2. NAMES   113

DEDICATED

TO ALL ITALIAN FILM MAKERS

WITH AFFECTION AND ADMIRATION

AND ESPECIALLY TO

ENRICO GUAZZONI

THE FIRST OF THE GREAT ITALIAN DIRECTORS

AND TO

ROBERTO ROSSELLINI

THE LATEST

AUTHOR'S FOREWORD

A list of those who have helped me in one way or another in the writing of this book would read like a directory of the Italian film industry. And since the more you strive to make a list complete the greater is the slight to the one person inadvertently omitted I propose to play for safety and thank in general, and without naming, the innumerable directors, producers, cameramen, journalists, publicity men and others who have helped me.

It would, however, be unforgivable not to mention my debt to two books, Il Romanzo del Cinema *by Vittorio Calvino, and* Storia del Cinema *by Francesco Pasinetti. Between them they provided an invaluable framework for a period of which I had no first-hand experience, a framework which I was able afterwards to fill in by conversations with people who had been active at those times.*

The English titles given in brackets after the Italian name of the film are in every case the most reasonably literal translation possible, and have been made without reference to any possibly existing titles in English for some of these films.

In giving the approximate sterling equivalent of figures quoted in lire I have followed the figures supplied by the Institute of Statistics, according to whom 100 lire in 1912 was equivalent to 366 in 1930, 621 in 1938, 5,250 in 9144 and 26,129 in 1948. The resulting figures have been turned into sterling at lire 2,000 equals £1, an approximately correct figure for 1948. All figures should therefore be considered in terms of 1948 values, a point of some importance. This method results in certain anomalies, of course, but any other system seemed too complicated for a book as unpretentious as this.

Chapter One

EARLY DAYS

THE year 1907 is a convenient date for beginning a study of the Italian cinema, for it was in that year that serious production began. Previous production had been largely in the hands of amateurs or dilettantes, but by this time it was clear that film production was about to move out of the category of an eccentric and sporadic activity and become big business.

The first steps had, however, been taken shortly before. It was in 1905 that two architects called Santoni and Alberini built a studio in the middle of that characteristic feature of the Roman landscape, the artichoke gardens, which were then as near the heart of the city as the Via Veio, just outside the Porta S. Giovanni. Two years later this had become Cines, a name that was to be synonymous with Italian production during its greatest periods and which was to remain in existence down to the outbreak of the Second World War.[1]

In 1906 an accountant called Arturo Ambrosio, who ran an optical shop in Turin, built a studio in partnership with a man called Pasquali. They equipped it in a manner that was considered the last word in technical ingenuity in those days, and a year later were in production. With commendable if surprising restraint their firm was christened simply Ambrosio.

Following, no doubt unconsciously, Mr. Cecil Hepworth, who in 1905 had produced *Rescued by Rover* at a cost of £7 14s. 9d., the first effort of Ambrosio was called *Il Cane Riconoscente* (*The Grateful Dog*), a title that indicates its content quite adequately. This precursor of the innumerable Rin-Tin-Tins and Lassies that have since delighted the dog-lovers

---

[1] Cines was revived in the autumn of 1949 as part of the campaign of State aid for the film industry. Together with Cinecitta, L.U.C.E., and F.N.I.C. (see Chapter Four) it represents the Government's more or less active participation in the industry.

11

of the world was rewarded by one of the earliest Oscars in cinematographic history, the Lumière Shield of Gold at the First Italian Cinematographic Competition.

Encouraged by their success the firm of Ambrosio launched out into
a positive spate of production, their early titles including *Nuccia La
Pecoraia* (*Nuccia the Shepherd Girl*), *Amore e Patria* (*Love and Country*),
Il Perdono del Nonno (*Grandfather's Pardon*) and *Ora Muoio Lieta*
(*Now I Die Happy*).

Ambrosio were amongst the first to use artificial light for shooting.
Though their studios had, in the fashion of the time, been built glass-
roofed to take advantage of the sunlight it was not long before, at the
instigation of Carlo Montuori,[1] the chief Italian cameraman, they
installed a quantity of the biggest street-lighting lamps that they could
find. They were delighted with the result, not so much because of any
artistic improvement in the films themselves, but because they could
now shoot practically regardless of the weather.

Also working in Turin at the same time was one of the pioneers of
cinema journalism and documentary. This was Rodolfo Omegna who
shot only 'film dal vero', or what in present-day jargon would be
called 'actuality'. Some of his efforts, notably *Il Terremoto di Messina*
(*The Messina Earthquake*) and *Caccia al Leopardo* (*The Leopard Hunt*),
were very successful. One of the main planks in any production platform at that period was, however, the comic film, and it was doubtless
because of the close affinity between Piemonte and France that many of
the most popular comedians of early Turin films were French. Prominent among them were Marcel Fabre, who was known as Robinet in
France and kept his stage name unchanged in Italy, André Deed, who
was known as Gribouille in France and changed to Cretinetti in Italy,
and Fernando Guillaume, who called himself Tontolini and later
Polidor.

During 1907 and 1908 producing houses were springing up like mush-
rooms. Many of the more prominent Italian industrialists of the time,
such as Fassini, Tempo, Sciamengo, Mecheri, Airoldi and di Robbiate
became interested in the new industry; Milan saw the birth of companies
called Armenia, Comerio, Milano and an Italian subsidiary of Pathé,
while in Rome, where the weather was more auspicious for production
than in Milan and Turin, which are notorious for their winter fogs and

---

[1] Carlo Montuori is still active ; he was the cameraman of Vittorio de Sica's *Ladri
di Biciclette* (*Bicycle Thieves*), made in 1948, and perhaps the best Italian post-war film.

spring and autumn mists and rains, were founded Italia, Nova, Celio, Savoia, Aquila, Fert and Tiber as well as a company that in later years was, with Cines, to be one of the twin colossi of Italian production— Caesar. Further south, in Naples, there was one single venture— Gustavo Lombardo's company, which bore his own name. It is one of the few names still represented at the present day, for old Lombardo's son, Goffredo Lombardo, runs the Roman studios called Titanus and the renting house with the same name.

Lombardo rather specialised in productions that were based on the countryside round Naples and its folk-lore, but in this he was in a minority, for the greater number of Italian producers soon decided that the proper genius of Italian production lay in historical and costume films. As early as 1908 and 1909 Cines had made a number of such films, of which *Catilina*, directed by Caserini, was the greatest success. Ancient Rome was only one of the periods to be exploited, however, and among other successful films of this period were *Giovanni dalle Bande Nere* (the name of a famous soldier of the Medici family) and *Anita Garibaldi* (the famous wife of the great political leader).

Even Shakespeare, who was not unknown as a writer of historical plays, was quickly laid under tribute, and Mario Caserini's version of *Macbeth* was rated very high by contemporary critics and sold well abroad. Every country of Europe, every period, provided grist for their insatiable mills, and titles of the period include *Schiavo di Cartagine* (*Carthaginian Slave*), *I Cavalieri della Morte* (*The Knights of Death*), directed by Edoardo Bencivenga (who was then one of the most successful and best known directors), *Brutus, Lucrezia Borgia* and *Hamlet.* One of the most popular, called *Sardanapalo* (*Sardanapalus*) was exactly 716 feet long, representing about ten minutes' screen time. In this form it won a prize at a cinema festival at Milan, and if any of the critics, who were at the Venice Festival in 1948 when *La Terra Trema* was plodding leadenly and inexorably towards its third hour, remembered *Sardanapalo*, sighs of nostalgia must have mingled with those of weariness.

Allowing for the technical crudities of production in those early years the level of artistry and taste reached in most of the historical subjects was remarkably high, a fact probably due to the background of the men who were then at the head of Italian production. This was very different from that of men in corresponding positions in America. In Italy at the head of Cines were the Marchese Ernesto Pacelli and

13

Barone Alberto Fassini ; Celio was run by Barone Alberto Blanc, Marchese Alberto del Gallo di Roccagiovane and Marchese Patrizi; the president of Tiber was Conte Enrico di S. Martino; and Barone Rodolfo Kanzler was one of the active heads of Palatino.

The presence of such men as these at the heads of the big Italian companies goes some way to explain not only the emphasis on historical spectacle but also the high standard to which these films were made, for they came from families going back with unbroken traditions into the Middle Ages. They lived, many of them, in the identical palaces in which the events that they filmed had taken place centuries before, and they had been accustomed from childhood to live amongst the buildings, costumes, pictures, statuary and furniture of the past. In some cases they still bore the same names as those of the ancestors whose deeds they were putting on the screens of the world.

One of the more enthusiastic and successful producers of that epoch was, for example, the Marchese di Bugnano, who divided his time between the cinema and politics, for he was a Questore for Naples and a Deputato in the Camera. At a time when many producers were still thinking in terms of the painted theatrical back-cloth, he was thinking in terms not inconsistent with the way in which the studios work to-day. He would hire the best architects in Italy to design his sets; he would furnish them, not out of the property room or the second-hand shop, but with the best that the finest furnishing and textile houses could design specially for the purpose; carpets, silver-ware, glass—all were genuine, and the best that could be found. Even butlers in his contemporary films were men who had been trained from boyhood to do in real life what he wanted depicted on the screen. In fact on more than one occasion he persuaded his aristocratic friends themselves to play the parts of extras in scenes laid in the social world in which they really moved.

It was also undoubtedly due to the calibre of the men at the head of the industry that reputable authors were willing to allow their work to be filmed, and even to write especially for the screen. Such writers as Testoni, Marco Praga, Luciano Zuccoli, Guido Gozzano, Lucio d'Ambra, Zorzi and Simoni, all well-known writers of the period, produced scenarios and dialogue for captions, or else sold the rights of their previously published work. After all, with d'Annunzio setting the example, who were they to hold back? Yet D'Annunzio gave his work to the screen not because he had any faith in the artistic possibilities

14

of the new medium, or even because he found it interesting, but simply because he needed the money.

In 1911 d'Annunzio sold Ambrosio the screen rights in all his existing works, and also undertook to let them have the rights to all his future works at a flat rate of 40,000 lire each (£5,200), a gratifying kind of blank cheque. In this way he became one of the most prolific sources of material for the Italian screen, such films as *La Nave* (The Ship), *La Figlia di Jorio* (*The Daughter of Jorio*), *Gioconda*, *Fiaccola Sotto il Moggio* (*The Light under the Bushel*), *Piacere* (*Pleasure*), *Giovanni Episcopo* and many others being based on his work.

The years 1910 and 1911 saw the tide of Italian historical films reach its flood. Mario Caserini followed up his success with *Catilina* by making *Lucrezia Borgia* with Maria Gasperini in the title role. It was about this time, too, that the star system first began to make itself felt. 1910 had seen Florence Lawrence emerge in America from her anonymity as The Biograph Girl, and 1912 saw the star system well established, with Pauline Bush, J. Warren Kerrigan, John Bunny and Flora Finch, and Alice Joyce. The best known Italian couple were Alberto A. Capozzi and Mary Cleo Tarlarini who had made a great success in Arrigo Ferrari's version of George Ohnet's *Romanzo di Un Giovane Povero* (*Romance of a Poor Young Man*), produced by Ambrosio under the title of *L'Ultimo dei Frontignac* (*The Last of the Frontignacs*); they also appeared together in *La Rose Rouge* (*The Red Rose*), in *Granatiere Roland* (*Roland the Grenadier*), and in *Convegno Supremo* (*Supreme Meeting*). This year, too, the first screen version of *Pinocchio*, Carlo Collodi's ever popular children's book, made its appearance in its first screen version, with the comedian Polidor in the name part. Parallel with this the usual films on classical themes were being made— Giuseppe de Liguoro producing versions of Homer's Odyssey and of Dante's Inferno, himself taking the parts of, respectively, Ulysses and Count Ugolino, while Piero Fosco appeared on the scene for the first time, making a film called *La Caduta di Troia* (*The Fall of Troy*).

Two of Mario Caserini's films in 1912 were Wagner's *Siegfried* and *Parsifal*, while the same year saw the first of d'Annunzio's many contributions to the screen, *Gioconda*, and *La Nave* (*The Ship*). A new star, Francesca Bertini, who within a few years was to dominate the Italian cinema, appeared opposite Amleto Novelli in Cines' *Rosa di Tebe* (*Rose of Thebes*).

Caserini was remarkable in these days both for his versatility and his

15

untiring output; at one time, indeed, it had been his boast to make a one-reel comedy in a single day. In 1913 he was responsible, among others, for a *Dante e Beatrice* (*Dante and Beatrice*), and for a film called *L'Amor Mio Non Muore* (*My Love Does Not Die*), starring the only couple that could rival Alberto A. Capozzi and Mary Cleo Tarlarini in popularity—Lyda Borelli and Mario Bonnard; the film was devoted to the sorrows and tribulations of life and love among the duchesses and princes of aristocratic Roman society, and was described, no doubt with perfect justice, as a melodrama.

But the real importance of 1913 is that it saw the first of the great spectacular films with which Italy was to make such an impression on the screens of the world. This was *Gli Ultimi Giorni di Pompei* (*The Last Days of Pompeii*). Ten thousand feet of film and over a thousand extras were devoted to making a worthy version of Bulwer Lytton's famous novel. It is interesting to note that even then the cycle in film making was appearing; in this year two versions of *The Last Days of Pompeii* were produced, one by Ambrosio and one by Pasquali, who had now left the firm that he had founded with Arturo Ambrosio to produce on his own account. This was to be repeated a little later when, in deadly rivalry, Caesar and Tiber produced simultaneously rival versions of *The Lady of the Camellias*. Out of the comparatively large output for this year the most notable films were the first version to be made of that Italian schoolroom classic *I Promessi Sposi* (*The Betrothed*), directed by Ubaldo del Colle and Ernesto Pasquali with costumes by Caramba, *Romanticismo* (*Romance*), of which Camillo de Riso was both director and star, *Giuseppe Verdi* directed by Giuseppe de Liguoro and *Giovanna d'Arco* (*Joan of Arc*), made by Nino Oxilia with Maria Jacobini in the principal part. A little later the same director and star made a religious film which created quite a minor sensation, *In Hoc Signo Vinces* (*With This Sign You Shall Conquer*).

Shortly after *The Last Days of Pompeii* came the second of the great Italian spectacular films—*Quo Vadis?*—which was finished early in 1913. The director was Enrico Guazzoni who from the days of his first entrance into the industry had shown a decided flair for costume films ; *Brutus*, which he had directed in 1910, had been very well received, and now he was to achieve the summit of his career, for although he remained in pictures at least down to 1943, when he directed the picture about Raphael's famous model and mistress *La Fornarina* (*The Bakeress*), he never afterwards achieved a comparable success.

16

Although *The Last Days of Pompeii* is entitled to its position as the first of these great spectacles, this is largely on account of its length and the masses of people deployed on the screen. But where *Quo Vadis?* made real innovations was in the construction of the enormous sets representing ancient Rome; nothing like this had ever been done, or even attempted, before. Guazzoni, like Griffith after him, was a human dynamo of energy and was the driving force in every department of the film. He himself designed the sets; he designed the costumes, hundreds and hundreds of them, for the actors and even the extras; he insisted on real lions for the circus scenes. Seeing the film nowadays one is left with three main impressions—that the physical apparatus of the film is excellent, its sets and costumes and buildings even now appearing more than adequate, that though the handling of the crowds is masterly the acting of the principals is strictly in the theatrical tradition of the time and makes no concession to the intimacy of the camera, and that many of the great scenes are thrown away, owing to the perfunctory manner in which, by modern standards, they are treated. But this is, of course, to view it out of its period, and it is necessary to see it alongside other contemporary productions to realise what a really remarkable achievement it was.

It was also an outstanding commercial success. It cost 48,000 lire (£6,940) to make, a great sum for those days, but it brought in at least ten times as much. It was in nine reels which, at the running speed of silent films, meant about two hours' playing time, and in America, where it had a great success, it paved the way for the policy which Griffith subsequently adopted by being shown not in the ordinary cinemas but in first class theatres which were taken for a season; this was the first time that any film had been handled in this way. The demand for prints was world-wide, for in those happy distant days not only was there no language barrier, but there were no quotas, no tariffs, and no currency restrictions. The staff of Cines were working for weeks on twenty-four hour shifts to keep up with the despatch of the prints for which the world was clamouring.

The success of *Quo-Vadis?* was still in full flood when work was started on its successor, *Cabiria*, produced by Giovanni Pastrone, directed by himself under his nom-de-plume of Piero Fosco, and written by Gabriele d'Annunzio himself. Pastrone had, in fact, begun his preparations as long ago as June 1912 when he went to Paris to do research for the film in the Carthaginian section of the Louvre Museum, a thing

B

which in itself indicates the unusual seriousness with which the thing was tackled. *Cabiria* was, considering the resources of the cinema at that time, a quite exceptional tour-de-force. Made with a disregard of cost and technical difficulties that had never been known before, it seemed the dizziest peak of the Italian cinema. Even nowadays *Cabiria* is still the symbol throughout the world of the cinema for the outstanding achievement of the early days before Griffith's great period.

Pastrone returned from his Parisian researches, and while the wardrobe people were hard at work on the costumes, he began to get his cast together. Italia Almirante Manzini, Umberto Mozzato, Casciano, Minolli, Vitaliano, Lydia Quaranta and many others of Italy's best-known actors were employed in long and painstaking tests and rehearsals. One story is typical: Pastrone would have nothing to do with false beards; one particular actor, already cast for a part that called for a long white beard, was paid for many months just to grow his own, with strict instructions that it was to be long, flowing, dignified and white.

Then, for the character called Maciste in d'Annunzio's script, Pastrone needed a large man, almost a giant, of exceptional strength. Pastrone spent months looking for a man suitable for this part; he interviewed by the hundred wrestlers from Paris, firemen from Milan, and porters from Trieste. Finally he found him; he was a docker at Genoa called Bartolomeo Pagano, herculean in stature and with an enormous grin. He could barely read and write, but that was unimportant. Pastrone signed him up, and in so doing made the fortune of the man who was to become one of Italy's most popular actors.

Maciste, who never used his own name again, had been earning 12 lire (19 shillings) a day as a docker; Pastrone offered him 20, and that was enough to decide Maciste. It is doubtful if, at that time, the giant ever imagined in his wildest dreams that in a few years he could be earning the fabulous sum of 750,000 lire (£97,500) a year. When the Italian industry reached the depths of its slump a few years later Maciste was one of the last actors to be paid off. The ending is at least a happy one, for Maciste, like the good Genoese that he was—the Genoese are always called the Scots of Italy—had saved his money and invested it sensibly. He retired into private life to enjoy the riches that fortune had dropped into his lap.

D'Annunzio wrote not only the story but also the captions, perhaps the only ones ever written by a major literary figure. Their merit is open to debate, and they were very numerous and very long. The sets were extremely complex, elaborate, and sumptuous, and for the first time the camera was put on a dolly and given freedom to roam about the stages. But what really took the public fancy was the extraordinarily painstaking reconstruction of a long-past period in all its lavish detail. The period was, of course, that of the Punic wars, once so well known to every schoolboy, down to the destruction of Carthage. The model work was excellent, the make-up first class, and artificial illumination was used on a large scale and with great success. The actual shooting took about seven months and the film cost the then enormous sum of 1,000,000 lire (£130,000). When it was presented at Milan it was accompanied by an orchestra of a hundred players performing the music specially composed for it by Ildebrando Pizzetti; this was said to·be extremely effective, especially the section called La Sinfonia del Fuoco which he had written for the scene which shows the terrible rites of those who worshipped Moloch; the emotional effect of this sequence was heightened even more by having the print coloured red by the use of an aniline dye.[1]

It must be admitted that many histories of the cinema, in paying to D. W. Griffith their well-deserved tributes, have sometimes been a little less than generous to his predecessors Guazzoni and Pastrone. Griffith himself, who had seen both films shortly before he began to plan *Birth of a Nation* and *Intolerance*, in fact while he was still at work on *Judith of Bethulia*, made no secret of the impression that they had made on him.

[1] An example followed by William Dieterle in 1949 for the last sequences in *Vulcano*.

Chapter Two

THE ARRIVAL OF THE STAR SYSTEM AND
PRODUCTION DURING THE FIRST WORLD WAR

THE spectacular film was not the only contribution that Italy made to the developing cinema of the early years of this century. Much more debatable in value was Italy's share in developing the star system, and its inevitable accompaniment—the 'fan'. The movement to identify popular players by name developed more or less simultaneously with America, where Florence Lawrence, John Bunny, Flora Finch, J. Warren Kerrigan, Alice Joyce and Pauline Bush were becoming known just about the time that Francesca Bertini, Lina Cavalieri, Alberto A. Capozzi and Mary Cleo Tarlarini, Emilio Ghione, Lyda Borelli, Mario Bonnard and, of course, Maciste were becoming popular names in Italy and France.

One of the earliest stars to show what the system was capable of producing if properly handled was Francesca Bertini. Her real name was Elena Vitiello, and although born in Florence she was in fact pure Neapolitan with the blackest of hair. Her mother was herself an actress, and the little Francesca was playing tiny parts in the dialect plays in which her parents specialised almost as soon as she could walk and talk. Her success on the stage seemed, however, likely to be always rather modest, her deep and throaty voice being unattractive by the standards of those days and oddly at variance with her youthful grace and fresh simplicity. It was, however, these latter qualities which caught the fancy of a cinema talent scout as in refreshing contrast to the *femme fatale* qualities of such actresses as Lyda Borelli, and he signed her up for Pathe Italiana, for whom she played a number of small parts without any startling success.

In 1912 she had her first big part, playing opposite one of the most

20

popular actors of the day, Amleto Novelli, in a Cines film called *Rosa di Tebe* (*Rose of Thebes*); she scored an instantaneous hit. Then came one of those odd quirks of fortune that do so much to make or mar a career. Tiber borrowed her from Cines, paying her 2,000 lire (£260) a a month, out of which she had to pay for her clothes: three years later she was to sign a contract with Caesar which would pay her 200,000 (£26,000) for a single film. Tiber, when they had finished her first film, liked it so much that they decided to keep her. Cines wanted her back. The result of the impasse was a lawsuit which may have done Tiber and Cines no particular good but was the making of Francesca Bertini, whose name was spread all over the newspapers for days and weeks on end.

She was fortunate, too, in her material, for this was a period when, following in the footsteps of d'Annunzio, good Italian writers did not think it beneath them to write for the screen. Her producers consistently chose subjects which gave full scope to her capacity for expressing southern passion, and her early films included *Don Pietro Caruso* and *Assunta Spina* (the latter was remade in Italy in 1947 by Mario Mattoli, with Anna Magnani in Francesca Bertini's part and that great actor Eduardo de Filippo opposite her), while among the young men who were busy gaining for themselves a foothold in the cinema by writing scripts for her was Augusto Genina, who was later to become one of Mussolini's favourite directors of propaganda films.

Borne along on a constant stream of films—*Malia, Sangue Blu* (*Blue Blood*), *Il Processo Clemenceau* (*The Clemenceau Trial*), *Tosca, Diana L'Affascinatrice* (*Diana the Fascinating*), *La Signora delle Camelie* (*The Lady of the Camellias*), *Odette, Fedora* were some of the titles—she rose to great heights of fame and popularity. Parisian dressmakers, coiffeurs and creators of perfume and millinery named their most glamorous achievements after her ; not surprisingly, she herself became capricious to the point of wantonness. She worked as, when and where she pleased.

In 1919, when the Italian industry was on the very eve of its decline, Francesca Bertini signed the largest contract that had ever been made up till that time—2,000,000 lire (£75,000) for eight films. But though she never saw the contract through, this is a story, like that of Maciste, that ends happily. In August 1921 they shot the last scene of *La Fanciulla di Amalfi* (*The Girl from Amalfi*), the third film to be made under the fabulous contract, and Francesca Bertini retired from the

21

screen for ever. With rare and praiseworthy good sense she retired while she was still young, attractive, and able to enjoy her very considerable wealth. She married into the Florentine nobility—a long step, especially in the Italy of the nineteen-twenties, from the Neapolitan dialect theatre which had been her cradle—and lived happily ever after.

During her active career Francesca Bertini reigned supreme but not unchallenged. Two other stars came within measurable distance of her. The first was Lina Cavalieri, whose statuesque beauty was in natural contrast to Francesca Bertini's slightly gamine vivacity. In 1913 Lina Cavalieri had reached such heights of popularity, abroad as well as in Italy, that her films were sold in America not only unseen, but in at least two cases before they were even made. In 1914, after hostilities had broken out, the American purchasers of her films did not feel that they could expose such a precious cargo to the hazards of war, so they sent a specially fast steamboat from America to carry her in speed and safety to the States. Not long after Lina Cavalieri signed a contract to make *La Storia di Manon Lescaut* in America.

Closest behind Lina Cavalieri in the race to challenge Francesca Bertini were Pina Menichelli, Lyda Borelli, Rina de Liguoro and Hesperia. Pina Menichelli, who began her working life as a seamstress, soon became one of the richest actresses in the world of that time, not so much because of her great box-office value (though of course this was considerable) but because of her extraordinary skill in extorting the utmost lira from any producer who wanted her services; if he began to show any signs of rebellion Pina Menichelli would promptly and ostentatiously begin to pack her numerous trunks preparatory to seeking her fortune abroad. That never failed to bring him to his senses. Her beauty was of a peculiarly voluptuous nature, and contemporary writers speak of 'her voluptuous fascination flowing in streams and torrents from her person'. Many of her films bore such titles as *Tigre Reale* (*Royal Tigress*), which indicate fairly clearly their nature, and it is perhaps worth recording that she also played in *La Seconda Moglie* (*The Second Wife*) which Amleto Palermi directed, and which was based on Pinero's *The Second Mrs Tanqueray*.

Lyda Borelli, also well up in the race, had perhaps the greatest influence on the girls and young women who formed her mass of admiring fans; so much so in fact that a special word, 'borellismo', was coined to describe the way in which they modelled themselves on her.

22

Girls just leaving school, young married women, shop girls, shorthand typists—they walked like her, did their hair like her, dressed as near to her style as their purses allowed, and whenever they found themselves within reach of a divan they reclined on it with the best imitation they could muster of her peculiarly languid grace. In many of her films she played opposite Mario Bonnard, who later became a director and as such made two of Anna Magnani's first three films; as a couple they were extremely popular, and their best-known film was *L'Amor Mio Non Muore* (*My Love Does Not Die*) directed by Mario Caserini in 1913. Lyda Borelli, who had come to the screen via the theatre, where she had played a long succession of smallish parts—perhaps it was this long apprenticeship that kept her from losing her head when her period of fantastic success arrived—bore no relation in private life to the *femme fatale* who brought her such fame and riches on the screen. She was a simple, good-hearted creature, and when she retired from the cinema she lived happily as the devoted wife of a Venetian business man.

Hesperia was perhaps of lesser stature than the others, but is worth commemorating if only for one of the more amusing incidents of the rivalry then so pronounced. In 1915 Caesar, for whom Francesca Bertini was then working, announced with a great fanfare of trumpets that she was going to play the name part in the most stupendous production of *The Lady of the Camellias* ever to be filmed. Nothing would content Hesperia but that she too should be a Lady of the Camellias, and so Tiber Film, who then 'owned' Hesperia, announced their even more stupendous production of *The Lady of the Camellias*. The actual productions raced neck and neck, and their opening nights were practically simultaneous. Caesar had their opening night at a cinema called the Moderno. Tiber, superlative-conscious to the last, had theirs at the Modernissimo. Hesperia's version was directed by Baldassare Negroni, one of the most prolific and successful directors of the period, who in 1921 directed Hesperia in *Madame Sans Gêne* and *Il Figlio di Madame Sans Gêne* (*The Son of Madame Sans Gêne*), both of which did very well in Europe.

Amongst the actors of this period two names stand out clearly above the others—Emilio Ghione and Bartolomeo Pagano who was never known by his own name but always as Maciste. Emilio Ghione was a slender, elegant, nervous, and extravagant young man who began as an extra working for Italia Film in Turin, in which capacity

23

he earned 90 lire (£12) a month. His first major success was in 1914 when he played opposite Francesca Bertini in *Storia di Un Pierrot* (*The Story of a Pierrot*), directed by Mario Costa. But his really great popularity began the following year when he created a character Za La Mort and himself directed the first film in which he appeared. Za la Mort was an apache, but a sentimental one. Living in the depths of the most squalid slums he was a sort of Robin Hood of the city, hating all that was brutal or oppressive, and robbing the rich to help and protect the poor and weak. In Za la Mort he created one of those characters which correspond, like Tarzan, so closely to some unfulfilled need in the ordinary myth-loving public that it is practically impossible to kill them off. Years later, in 1921 if not later, he was still making Za la Mort films, though every so often he would relent, as when in 1917 he again played opposite Francesca Bertini in a film of Roberto Bracco's play, *Don Pietro Caruso*.

From 1915 onwards he earned fabulous sums—he himself admitted to receiving 100,000 lire (£13,000) a month in 1915—and lived like a Renaissance prince. Extremely generous by nature he distributed largesse far and wide; but when the post-war crisis reached its climax his life declined into a melancholy oblivion. Forgotten by his one-time legion of admirers he worked in small revue companies until, years later, ill, worn out, and old before his time, he ended up in the charity ward of a Turin hospital; there, after some months of a painful and lingering illness, he died, a sad ending for a man who had formerly been the adored and elegant idol of the cinema public.

Maciste's story is both simpler and happier. His discovery by Pastrone has already been told, and Maciste was, of course, the real forerunner of Tarzan. The formula was simple in the extreme. Maciste was always a very good, very strong man, who was confronted by the most frightful of physical dangers which he overcame entirely by the use of his great physical strength. The very titles of his films, as so often, tell one exactly what they were like: *Maciste Contro la Morte* (*Maciste Against Death*), *Maciste all' Inferno* (*Maciste in Hell*), *Maciste contro Lo Sceicco* (*Maciste versus the Sheik*), *Maciste nella Gabbia dei Leoni* (*Maciste in the Lions' Den*), *Il Gigante della Dolomiti* (*The Giant of the Dolomites*); what is a little surprising is the calibre of the directors of these formula pictures—Guido Brignone, Mario Camerini (this was obviously an apprentice assignment for the man who from 1930 to 1948 was one of the best Italian directors), Carlo Campogalliani and

24

others. Like Francesca Bertini and Lyda Borelli he saved his money and retired in good order when the cinema no longer wanted him.

One of the effects of the rise of the star was, of course, enormously to emphasise the importance of the film as a vehicle to exploit a screen personality, with a corresponding diminution of interest in the great spectacular films where the individual star was necessarily subordinated to the sweep of history and the movements of masses of soldiers, panic-stricken mobs and volcanic eruptions.

The Za la Mort series has already been mentioned, as well as the Maciste epics; another very popular series was the *Topi Grigi* (*Grey Mice*) series.

One of the most successful producers and directors of this period was Baldassare Negroni, whose usual stars were Francesca Bertini, Alberto Collo and Emilio Ghione. One of his first films to have an outstanding success was the *Storia di Un Pierrot* referred to above, in which a new name, Leda Gys, made her appearance alongside Francesca Bertini and Emilio Ghione: this was followed by *Retaggio d'Odio* (*Inheritance of Hate*) with Maria Carmi. In 1915, the year after he made *Storia di Un Pierrot*, he directed the Hesperia version of *The Lady of the Camellias*, following this up in 1921 with the two Hesperia *Madame Sans Gêne* pictures. In 1926 he was directing Maciste films; and after that his name is less prominent.

One of the outstanding successes of the war years was *Sperduti nel Buio* (*Lost in the Dark*), a film which, like the contemporary and equally successful *Il Fuoco* (*The Fire*) of Piero Fosco, made a brave attempt to break away from the lazy and disastrous habit of using a long succession of captions to replace the search for the eloquent and evocative image. *Sperduti nel Buio* was directed by Nino Martoglio in 1914, and the principal players were Giovanni Grasso, Virginia Balistrieri, Maria Carmi and Dillo Lombardi. The framework of the story is that of parallel and contrasted stories, a method which D. W. Griffith was to use with greater richness and resource when, two years later, he made *Intolerance*. In *Sperduti nel Buio* one story is laid in the rich luxurious and carefree world of the aristocracy; the other in the squalid distress and preoccupations of the slums. The sets, in fact the whole physical apparatus of the film, were well devised, but the contrast remains too transparently a dramatist's device to harrow the emotions, and the direction, or, not to be too precise, the combination of direction and

25

acting, was too much in the bad old tradition of mouthing and ranting to bring the poor-good and decadent-rich characters to life.

Such films as these formed one of the two main currents of Italian production from the years from 1914 to the early post-war period. There was, however, one individual film that falls into no particular category, *Cenere* (*Ashes*), in which in 1916 Eleonora Duse made her one and only appearance on the screen in a version made at the Ambrosio studios in Turin of Grazia Deledda's novel of the same name. Her acting in this film is remarkable for its poise and restraint.

The other main current was a continuation, though never very successful, of the great Italian tradition of spectacle. In 1913 Guazzoni tried to follow up the success of his *Quo Vadis?*, making in that year both *Giulio Cesare* (*Julius Caesar*) and *Marcantonio e Cleopatra* (*Antony and Cleopatra*); Amleto Novelli played Caesar, and also Antony to Gianna Terribili Gonzales's Cleopatra. In both films, however, the acting was of less importance than the spectacle, as was usual in Guazzoni's work. In 1917 he was responsible for two more, *Gerusalemme Liberata* (*Jerusalem Freed*), based on Tasso's poem, and *Fabiola* from Cardinal Wiseman's famous novel. It is, in passing, interesting to note the element of repetition that is very strongly marked in the spectacular tradition of the Italian cinema; at least five versions of *Quo Vadis?* were made at one time or another, as well as two or three of *Gli Ultimi Giorni di Pompei* ; the latter and *Fabiola* have both been remade in Italy in 1948 by the new Italian company Universalia, while a joint American-Italian version of *Quo Vadis?* is being planned for 1950.

Others, too, did their best to follow the great but fading tradition. In 1919 Leopoldo Carlucci began to cater for those who still hankered after the enormous sets of old, the hundreds of extras, the feasts and the leopards, the dancing girls and the antique costumes, the toppling towers and the battling elephants, and made *Teodora*, while Caramba brought *I Borgia* (*The Borgias*) to the screen. In 1920 Guazzoni competed with *Il Sacco di Roma* (*The Sack of Rome*), and in 1922 he made his last great effort with *Messalina* which recalled not inadequately the glories of his great days, but had only a moderate success.

Guazzoni remained an active director until well into the Second World War. In 1939 he made *Il Suo Destino* (*His Destiny*); in 1940 *Antonio Meucci* and *Ho Visto Brillare Le Stelle* (*I Have Seen The Stars Shine*); in 1941 *La Figlia del Corsaro Verde* (*The Daughter of the Green*

26

Pirate), Oro Nero (Black Gold), and *I Pirati della Malesia (The Pirates of the Malay);* and finally in 1943 *La Fornarina.*

His career in many ways resembles that of D. W. Griffith, though his active life in the cinema was much longer. After a comparatively brief apprenticeship he developed suddenly the possession of his full powers, exerted his influence over a comparatively short period, and then seemed unable ever again to strike a properly creative vein.

Chapter Three

THE YEARS AFTER THE FIRST WORLD WAR

THE early post-war years saw the formation of two new producing
houses each of which has some importance for the light it
throws on either the artistic ideas or the economic conditions of
those times.

The first of these was Tespi, which was founded in 1919 by Arnaldo
Frateili, Umberto Fracchia and Luigi Pirandello. Pirandello had for
some time been interested in the cinema; indeed his novel *Si Gira*, which
was published in Italy in 1916 and later in England under the title
Shoot, deals with the life of a cameraman. As might be expected the
firm had a strongly literary bias, though one of their earliest productions, *Pantera di Neve* (*The Panther of the Snows*), which they made
in 1919 was a purely commercial film and as melodramatic as its title
would indicate. It was directed by Frateili, and Pirandello acted as
adviser. Very soon, however, they began to tackle more serious pro-
jects. In 1920 Frateili made *Una Notte Romantica* (*A Romantic Night*)
which was based, in spite of its title, on a story by Edgar Allan
Poe. Other productions of theirs included *La Scala di Seta* (*The
Silken Staircase*) from Luigi Chiarelli's comedy; a film of Balzac's
Cesar Birotteau starring Gustavo Salvini; *L' Indiana* (*The Indian Girl*)
which Umberto Fracchia based on a George Sand novel; *La Bella e La
Bestia* (*The Beauty and the Beast*) which was taken from an original
story of Fracchia's, and, perhaps most interesting of all, a film based
on Pirandello's own *La Rosa* (*The Rose*) with Bruno Barilli, Olympia
Barroero and Lamberto Picasso in the principal parts.

In 1922 a number of Italian producing houses decided that unity
might well be strength, and banded themselves together under the
title of Unione Cinematografica Italiana. They felt that only by

28

combining their financial and technical resources could they offer effective competition to the new American and German companies which were beginning to press them hard, not only in their export market but even at home. Another factor that induced them to combine was the feeling that the extremely high salaries which Italian stars had been getting was at least partly due to the feverish competition of rival producers for their services. After a few trial films they set about making a masterpiece in the traditional Italian manner; this was to be yet another version of *Quo Vadis?* to be produced by Arturo Ambrosio who had just been preparing himself by making *Teodora*. Their plan for *Quo Vadis?* was not only to kindle the flames of old glories by sympathetic magic, but to add to the technical strength and the star appeal of their films by large-scale importations. The German director Georg Jacoby was brought in to do again what Guazzoni had done so superbly before and was given Gabriellina d'Annunzio to help him; Kurt Courant came as cameraman and was given two Italians, Giovanni Vitrotti and Alfredo Donnelli, to assist him. Emil Jannings was signed up for the part of Nero and amongst the other actors and actresses were Rina de Liguoro, who had played Messalina in the film of that name, Elga Brink, Elena Sangro, Andrea Habay, Lilian Hall Davis, Alfonso Fryland, Edmondo van Riel and Gino Viotti. Money flowed like water, but the results were very moderate, whether considered from an artistic or from a commercial point of view.

At this stage there began a steady exodus of Italian talent, both acting and productive. Lina Cavalieri had already gone to Hollywood, and Tullio Carminati followed her; Carminati, who had once been La Duse's leading man on the stage, and had become one of the most popular of the young Italian stars, was still working in 1948 when, among other things, he played parts in two British films made partly in Italy—John Sutro's *The Glass Mountain*, directed by Henry Cass, and John Stafford's *The Golden Madonna*, directed by Vajda. Augusto Genina, who had graduated from writing to direction and production, went to work in Germany and France; Mario Bonnard and Carmine Gallone went to Germany, where Carmen Boni and Marcella Albani had preceded them and were having a considerable success; Livio Pavanelli, Righelli and Maria Jacobini went to Paris; Aldo Manetti, who had been one of the first to go, changed his name in America to Arnold Kent and, after a brief success, was killed in an automobile accident.

This was a period of the kind which has recurred from time to time in the film history of most countries, when the dominance of foreign productions is so great that the lack of any secure domestic market makes it extremely difficult for the producer to continue. In the early 'twenties in Italy no less than 68 per cent of the screen time was taken up by American films, 26 per cent by that of other countries, leaving only 6 per cent of Italian screen time for their own films, obviously an impossible position and one not unlike that current in England before we brought in the first Quota Act.

It may not be strictly relevant but it would be a pity not to recall the adventures of Alberto Rabagliati, and this is perhaps as good a place as any. About this time Fox ran a great competition with a deafening brou-ha-ha of publicity to select the best new Italian actor and actress to go to Hollywood. The competition was won by Marcella Battellini and Alberto Rabagliati. What happened to Signorina Battellini is not on record, but Alberto committed the tactical error of winning the affection of the 'fiancée' of a film magnate who may have been less virilely beautiful than Alberto but who was considerably more important. Even in those distant days the black list functioned with considerable efficiency, and Alberto found that every studio was barred to him, presumably for un-American activities, and he returned not too regretfully to Italy. At least that is his story as told with considerable gusto in his own *Quattro Anni fra le Stelle* (*Four Years among the Stars*), and who are we to doubt him?

The early 'twenties saw Italian production much reduced in quantity as well as in quality. From 1924 onwards, largely due to the horrid warning provided by the latest *Quo Vadis?*, it was extremely difficult to raise adequate capital, and in the years between 1924 and 1928 almost the only productions of note were a film of Carmine Gallone called *La Cavalcata Ardente* (*The Fiery Foray*) starring Soava Gallone, Emilio Ghione and Edmondo van Riel—in 1948 Carmine Gallone was directing *La Leggenda di Faust* for Rabinovitch in Rome—Mario Almirante's *L'Arzigogolo* (defined by the dictionary as *A Sophisticated Quibble*) from a Sem Benelli play of the same name, and *L'Uomo Più Allegro di Vienna* (*The Liveliest Man in Vienna*) which Amleto Palermi made with Ruggero Ruggeri and Maria Korda.

In 1926 an altogether new element came into the picture. Some of the American companies decided to produce in Europe, and in the van was Henry King to shoot in Italy *Romola* and *The White Sister*. Once

30

again the odd element of repetition in the pattern crops up, for after the Second World War the first American director to make a full scale American-standard film in Italy was the same Henry King, this time making *Prince of Foxes* with Tyrone Power, Orson Welles, Eva Breuer, Wanda Hendrix, Felix Aylmer, Everett Sloane and Leslie Bradley.

Romola and *The White Sister* were to be followed by another colossal spectacle, to be made in Italy with American money and under American direction. The subject chosen was *Ben Hur*, Lewis Wallace's then enormously popular historical novel which had already been filmed once by Kalem in 1917. This, however, had been a comparatively modest effort, and what was obviously in the American mind was a spectacle on a scale that would bear comparison with the best work of Guazzoni, Pastrone and Griffith. What turned their minds in this direction is a little difficult to say; it may have been the influence of the German screen, then very great in Hollywood—Murnau and Dupont were already under contract to American companies—with its emphasis on grandeur and masses; it may have been the hand of Cecil B. de Mille grasping after large-scale splendours. What is clear is that the whole thing was planned with the utmost seriousness; the great glory that had been Rome was to live again. The Circus Maximus was to be rebuilt, the Forum and the Palatine reconstructed.

Charles Brabin was chosen to direct it, George Walsh to play the title rôle, with Gertrude Olmsted, Francis X. Bushman and Kathleen Key in the principal parts; the entire company came to Italy. Then came one of those periodic upheavals that distinguish the life of film companies, this time an upheaval so great that its repercussions had disastrous effects in Italy. Brabin was recalled and replaced by Fred Niblo; Walsh was replaced by Ramon Novarro and Gertrude Olmsted by May McAvoy. In the upshot every foot of film that had been shot in Italy was discarded and the film entirely remade in America.

Commercially the decision was abundantly justified by events, for even so *Ben Hur* was one of the great all-time financial successes of the cinema, but it dealt a disastrous blow to any hope which the Italians may have entertained of American production in Italy being on such a scale as to make up, at least from the point of view of the technicians, workmen and extras, for the loss of domestic production. In the American mind production in Italy was, not unnaturally, associated with enormous and fruitless expense, and it was not indeed until some little time after the Second World War that the experiment

31

was repeated, this time with Gregory Ratoff's *Black Magic* and Henry King's *Prince of Foxes*, as well as a number of more modest ventures. Fortunately all seems to have gone well this time, and there is a reasonable hope that American production in Europe on a fair scale will continue to the mutual benefit of the Americans and ourselves, and possibly with the highly desirable result of better films all round.

In 1926, when the Italian cinema industry was already feeling that it might as well give up altogether, Warner Brothers launched the sound film, to be followed a year later by the talking pictures. One man, however, was determined that at least there should be no premature burial of the Italian industry, in which he was convinced there were still signs of life. He set about the herculean task of resuscitation. This was Stefano Pittaluga, who had entered the industry as a renter, distributing both Italian and foreign films; he now determined to move into production, and set up an organisation called, with that typically Italian passion for initials, S.A.S.P.; this was the second of the two ventures to which the opening sentence of this chapter refers. It was also at the precise moment when Amleto Palermi, with that perpetual desire for a return to past achievements, had decided to make yet another *Last Days of Pompeii*, to be directed by Carmine Gallone and to star Maria Korda, Victor Varconi and Bernard Goetzke, stars chosen specially with the all-important German market in view. Pittaluga set up his headquarters in Turin, perhaps a symbolic gesture since that had been the birthplace of the Italian cinema, and one of his first acts was to send one of his cameramen, Massimo Terzano, to Africa to take scenes of an expedition there.

Very few of the films produced during the years 1926 to 1928 are worth even recording, but perhaps a place may be made for Genina's version of Rostand's *Cyrano de Bergerac* with Pierre Magnier and Linda Moglia, and Baldassare Negroni's *Beatrice Cenci* with Maria Jacobini. Almost the only other film that in any way stood out was Mario Camerini's *Kiff Tebbi* (*As You Please*); this was based by Luciano Doria on a novel of the same name by Luciano Zuccoli, and starred Donatella Neri, Marcello Spada and Ugo Gracci; the main points of interest about it are that all the exterior scenes for this film of colonial life were shot on location in Africa, a thing that was comparatively rare in those days (it may even have been the first faint forerunner of the new Italian realism which, stifled under Fascism, flowered in its post-war renaissance in 1945 and the following years), and that it was made by a

32

co-operative organisation called A.D.I.A., which stands for Autori Direttori Italiani Associati.

Curiously enough the last two years of the silent film in Italy, at a time when one might not unreasonably have expected the industry to be more than ever moribund, produced a sudden revival of activity, a kind of dying rally. This was due in large measure to Alessandro Blasetti and a small group of like-minded young men who gathered round him—Sarandrei, Solaroli, Comin, Masetti, Medin, Solito and some others. Blasetti founded a journal called *Cinematografo* in the columns of which there was waged a sprightly and unceasing warfare on S.A.S.P., Pittaluga himself and the journals which supported him. Guglielmo Giannini, who later became famous as the founder and leader of the Uomo Qualunque party, and who at that time had a more restricted fame as the editor of *Kines*, a trade weekly, became involved in the controversy too.

To summarise, briefly and inadequately, the point of view of the Blasetti party, one could say that they maintained that the rehashing of old formulae, the attempt always to make pictures that were commercially safe (a policy to which, after his first brave beginning, Pittaluga had become increasingly committed) was a policy of negation and despair, and that only by finding subjects and treatments that were fresh and essentially Italian, with some proper relation to the life of the present day, could the Italian cinema industry hope for salvation.

After two years of controversy and preparation Blasetti and his associates prepared to put their theories to the proof. With the support of, principally, Stefano Sanjust di Teulada and Marchese Roberto Lucifero, Blasetti founded Augustus, and by the beginning of 1929 had completed his first film, the screenplay of which he had written himself with the collaboration of Aldo Vergano, who was also later to become a director. The film was called *Sole* (*Sun*), and the cast included Dria Paola, Marcello Spada, Vasco Creti and Vittorio Vaser. It is a film that, during the Fascist period, was widely hailed as the first adequate celebration of the Fascist spirit to reach the screen. But this is probably a little unfair to Blasetti, for the subject of the film was the reclamation of marshes and waste land, and the lives of those engaged in the work, one of the good and positive achievements of Fascism. Technically rather uneven, it was acted with unusual restraint (perhaps, though he would not have dared to admit it, Blasetti had learned

33

something from the makers of *Earth*, *The General Line* and other great silent Russian films on analogous themes) and contained a number of sequences that were visually of very considerable beauty. It seems a little incongruous that a film hailed as the first Fascist film should have been silent, so that all that wild and whirling rhetoric, all that grandiose imagery, had to be reduced to some gestures and a few captions. At any rate it was shown privately to Mussolini before its public release, and duly received the blessing of Il Duce's approval.

At the same time that Blasetti was making *Sole*, Mario Camerini was at work on *Rotaie* (*Rails*); his cameraman was Ubaldo Arata who was later to do such magnificent work on *Roma, Citta Aperta* (*Rome, Open City*), and the cast included Maurizio d'Ancora, Kathe von Nagy and Daniele Crespi. This was the first serious film that Camerini had made (his previous efforts had all been Macistes, or something similar), and it already showed the beginnings of what was to become the smooth and economical style of the director who subsequently made *Due Lettere Anonime* (*Two Anonymous Letters*), *La Figlia del Capitano* (*The Captain's Daughter*) and *Molti Sogni per Le Strade* (*The Street has Many Dreams*). *Rotaie* was shot as a completely silent film, but it was afterwards dubbed with a sound track, though this was limited to music, effects and one or two snatches of dialogue.

The whole of the story is centred on a young couple, their long search for work, and their eventual success. The film was distinguished by a number of happy touches, and the recurring contrast between the lives of the poor and the rich is done with comprehension, sympathy and adequate subtlety. Typical are the railway scenes, alternating between the first class carriages, with their luxury but their reserved and frigid atmosphere, and the warm humanity and crowded discomfort of the third class carriages on the same train, with mothers suckling their babies and a little boy shyly offering an apple to the girl who, with her sweetheart, is running away from the Riviera hotel where they have been staying; memorable, too, is the face of the young man when he is losing at roulette, the atmosphere of the railway stations, especially at night, and of the rush of the train through the countryside.

Chapter Four

THE COMING OF SOUND AND THE
FASCIST PERMEATION OF THE CINEMA

THE sound film took four years to make the journey from Hollywood to Rome. At the time when the advent of sound filled the minds of the cinema magnates of all nations with panic, the Italian industry was very decidedly in a state that might be mortal illness or might be protracted convalescence, but was certainly not health. A sudden shock, it was felt, might prove fatal. However the patient managed, by some means or other, to weather the first few years, and Stefano Pittaluga, who had the doctor's mandate, decided that sound had come to stay and that Italy must follow the American example as soon as possible.

By this time Pittaluga had moved the scene of his activities to Rome, taking over the old Cines studios, and it was here that the first Italian sound film was made. It was called, not one feels untypically, *La Canzone dell' Amore* (*The Song of Love*) and was directed by Gennaro Righelli. It starred Dria Paola, who had been such a great success in *Sole*, and Elio Steiner. The date was 1930.

The making of the film had been far from easy. Though new Western Electric equipment had arrived from America there was an almost total lack of trained technicians who knew anything about the new medium. But there was plenty of goodwill and determination, plus that amazing Italian talent for improvisation, and Righelli and his recordist Vittorio Trentino succeeded in turning out a very reasonable job. In fact they did so well that French and German versions were called for.

Naturally the plenitude of Italian music, songs and opera provided a great wealth of raw material for sound films, and films of this kind have ever since been a major part of Italian production. Santa Lucia

35

and Marechiaro were in the years to come to be an inexhaustible mine for these films and it is interesting to note that even in 1948 a complete Italian sound film, made by Romana Film, directed by Guido Brignone, and starring a popular Neapolitan singer, Eva Nova, was reputedly made for a total cost of lire 16,000,000 (£8,000).

The second Italian sound film was *La Vecchia Signora* (*The Old Lady*). This was made by Caesar, now controlled by Guiseppe Barattolo who had been the producer in silent days of Francesca Bertini's last films, and was made almost simultaneously with *La Canzone dell' Amore*.[1] The arrival of the talking film had in Italy much the same initial effect as in other countries—the inability of the old-time silent actors to cope with the new demands led to an influx of theatrical talent, and this, naturally, to a temporary emphasis on productions that were photographed stage plays rather than films proper. Of this genre were *Rubacuori* (*Stealer of Hearts*), made in 1931 and starring Armando Falconi, and *Corte d'Assise* (*Court of Assize*) made the previous year by the same director Guido Brignone. Even the great comic actor Ettore Petrolini made his début in the new medium with three films, the best of which was *Medico per Forza*, an adaptation of Molière's *Medecin Malgre Lui* which had been one of his traditional stage successes.

The advanced wing, still led by Blasetti, was far from being satisfied with this unimaginative use of the great new possibilities of sound, but their first efforts to take some intelligent and resourceful advantage of the new developments were not altogether successful, neither Blasetti's *Resurrectio* (*Resurrection*) nor Anton Giulio Bragaglia's *Vele Ammainate* (*Furled Sails*) being more than mediocre. But these were prentice efforts, and they soon began to improve; for example Blasetti's *Terra Madre* (*Mother Earth*) which starred Leda Gloria, Sandro Salvini and Isa Pola. Although the story was rather banal— a nobleman who had abandoned his estates is forced by circumstances to return to them—Blasetti succeeded in catching the atmosphere and feeling of the countryside very well, and in getting unusually restrained

---

[1] *La Vecchia Signora* was directed by Amleto Palermi; and in the cast were Emma Gramatica, Maurizio d'Ancora and Vittorio de Sica; this is one of the first recorded appearances of the man who was later to become one of Italy's finest and most sensitive actors, and widely known in England and America as the director of *Sciuscia* and *Ladri di Biciclette*. One of the outstanding points in the film, especially remarkable in view of its early date, is the counterpoint between sound and image achieved in the carriage drive scene. The music was by Umberto Mancini.

and natural performances from his cast. Even more to the point, however, were Camerini's next two films, *Figaro e La Sua Gran' Giornata* and *Gli Uomini Che Mascalzoni*.

Figaro e La Sua Gran' Giornata (*Figaro's Great Day*) was made in 1931 and starred Gianfranco Giachetti, Leda Gloria, and Maurizio d'Ancora. Taken from a comedy by Arnaldo Fraccaroli called *Ostrega che Sbrego*, it is laid in the Veneto of the nineteenth century, and Camerini, more than living up to the promise he had shown in *Rotaie*, showed his ability in pinning down the atmosphere and manners of an Italian province with sympathy and humour; the arrival at a little station in the Veneto of an almost Emett-like train which solemnly halts at a level-crossing to give precedence to a horse and cart, the whims of a baritone, the consequences of a singer's failure to turn up for a concert and a performance of Rossini's *Barber* are some of a number of episodes, all close to nineteenth century provincial life, which he created with nice invention, light touch and lively wit.

Of more significance to the gradually developing Italian tradition was his next film: *Gli Uomini Che Mascalzoni* (*What Rascals Men Are*); this, by succeeding abroad largely because it was so genuinely and unforcedly Italian, went some way towards proving the truth of what Blasetti had been arguing in the days of the ' Cinematografo ' polemics, a theory which the post-war success of such films as *Sciuscia*, *Quattro Passi fra le Nuvole* and *Vivere in Pace* has again endorsed. The scene of *Gli Uomini Che Mascalzoni* was laid in the grounds of the Milan fair, and the screen-play, which marks one of the first appearances in the cinema world of Mario Soldati, who wrote it in collaboration with Camerini, was sentimental, but pleasantly so, and directed with a noticeably light touch. The stars, Vittorio de Sica, Lia Franca and Cesare Zoppetti, seemed happier and more at ease than in any previous Italian sound film.

The idea was taken a stage further with Blasetti's next film, *Palio*. Based on a musical comedy by Liugi Bonelli and starring Guido Celano and Leda Gloria, the film is laid in Siena during that fantastic period when, twice a year, the whole city goes mad over the traditional horse race round the city square, a subject for intense and burning rivalry between the various contrade, or parishes, of Siena. Blasetti was at great pains to recapture the characteristic feverish atmosphere of the place during this period, sketching it in with many little touches and subtleties which were sometimes at odds with the rather solid comedy provided by Bonelli. But although uneven, it has some magnificent moments, particularly those at the end of the film with the camera alternating between the frenzied crowd jamming every inch of the square where the most exciting race in the world is being run, and the quiet deserted streets at the other end of the city, where, pacing alone, is the figure of a woman distracted because she fears that her lover is one of the riders in this dangerous race.

During these first few years of the sound film the contribution of Caesar and the other houses were slight, and Cines, controlled by Emilio Cecchi after Pittaluga's departure, kept in production almost alone. Cecchi's intention was to lift Cines out of the rut into which it had fallen in its efforts to make the sole criterion of a film its probable commercial success; as so often happens they frequently failed to achieve even that, proving once again that if you only aim low enough you can be fairly sure of missing the target. As part of his plan Cecchi initiated the production of a series of ambitious documentaries, amongst them Blasetti's *Assisi*, Umberto Barbaro's *Cantieri dell' Adriatico* (*Shipyards of the Adriatic*), Raffaello Matarazzo's *Littoria e Mussolinia di Sardegna*, Ivo Perilli's *Zara*, F. M. Poggioli's *Paestum*, and *Il Ventre della Citta* (*The Belly of the City*) directed by Francesco di Cocco with music by Mario Labroca. These bear a very strong resemblance to the documentaries being made at the present time, for the Italian tradition in documentary, as will be seen in a later chapter, is very different from the British.

In 1932 came the first film which can genuinely be described as Fascist propaganda. This was *L'Armata Azzurra* (*The Army in Blue*), which was directed by Gennaro Righelli. Intended purely as a propaganda film to acclaim Mussolini's much publicised Air Force, it cost a great deal of time and money, and contained episodes, characters and songs that were oddly at variance with its ostensible theme. These were then considered to detract from the more solid merits of the propaganda sections, though the verdict would now be different. The editing was done by Giorgio Simonelli, who made good use of his experience by directing shortly afterwards a workmanlike documentary on the same topic, called *Aeroporto del Littorio*.

Of the productions of these first few years perhaps one other is worth recording, *Il Suo Bambino* (*Her Baby*) made by Caesar. It was a remake by Friedrich Feher of a film which he had previously directed in Germany, with some of the scenes shot in Prague; the actors included

38

Feher himself, Magda Sonia and Hans Heher as the 'bambino' of the title. The film is rather long, but what is of merit is the unusually imaginative use of sound; in the picturisation of a group of houses on the outskirts of a great city it blends nicely the noises drifting softly in from the city, the cry of a child, the chattering of the women, the faint sound of a barrel organ that stops a mother from going to sleep. Well handled, too, are the scenes shot in a doss-house, and the sequence which shows a child alone and lost, a situation in which his emotions of loneliness and fright have been found a subtle visual form.

Newsreels are, of course, almost as old as the industry. Topical items were included in Lumière's original programme in 1890, and in 1897 there was actually a news reel cinema open in Paris run by Alexander Rapoutat, while for some time in 1906 Will Barker's *London Day by Day* ran at the old Empire Music Hall with considerable success. In Italy one of the principal purveyors of news in celluloid was an organisation called L'Istituto Nazionale L.U.C.E.

Originally founded as an organisation whose function was to make documentaries and didactic and educational films outside the scope of the commercial companies, L.U.C.E. had become increasingly a vehicle for Fascist propaganda. The potentialities of the film as a propaganda medium were, however, much more apparent when in 1930 L.U.C.E. became the proud possessors of three mobile recording trucks; from that time on it was a very lucky cinema patron indeed who, at some time or other in the programme, did not find the Duce's voice blaring out from the loudspeaker behind the screen as he cut the first sod on a housing or reclamation project, reviewed his mighty troops, helped to get in the harvest, or just orated from some balcony.

Like most other dictatorship regimes the Fascists were fascinated by the film industry. They saw in it, rightly enough, a propaganda channel of immense value; they thought, as usual, that they could make this channel serve their ends. All the less reputable elements, who were neither few, timid, nor lacking in resource, were attracted by what seemed to be the enormous possibilities for personal advantage, ranging from financial graft to an unlimited choice of pretty girls.

Even though it means departing from the chronological order of events, it will be more convenient to consider here the whole story of Fascist intervention in the cinema industry, even though we must go as far forward as 1942. It would be difficult to consider separately the extraordinarily complicated financial structures which the Fascist

39

Government proceeded to erect with the intention of encouraging the expansion of film production in Italy, and of ensuring Italian films a return that would, at least on paper, make the industry solvent, and would control the competition set up by foreign films.

The first plank in the platform was the founding in 1935 of the Direzione Generale per la Cinematografia; this was a part of the Ministero per la Cultura Popolare, universally known in those days as 'Minculpop'.

The second plank was the opening of a Sezione Cinematografica (Films Section) of the Banca del Lavoro, a banking institution which had been set up by the Fascist State to provide finance for those undertakings which the State wished to encourage and for which private capital was either inadequate or, for one reason or another, shy in coming forward. The Sezione Cinematografica was authorised to advance part of the capital, not exceeding 60 per cent, of any film of whose making it approved; the cases in which they advanced less than 60 per cent were usually those in which the reasons for making the film had not been advanced with, shall we say, sufficient persuasiveness.

In exceptional cases—*Scipione L'Africano* was one—they would even advance the whole of the necessary capital; and if, when the film was finished, it was considered to have artistic or ideological value, then the producers were as a reward excused the repayment of a part of the capital advanced by the Sezione Cinematografica.

The producers thus had every advantage. Either the film was popular and made a profit at the box office (which was good), or if it failed to make a profit, this was because it had rare artistic qualities too fine to be widely appreciated and so producers paid back only part of the capital that had been advanced (which again was good). Or, sometimes, the Sezione Cinematografica could be persuaded that the film had artistic and possibly ideological values in spite of having done well at the box office, in which case producers not only made a profit but were also excused from re-paying some of the capital (which was best of all).

The third plank in the platform was a sliding scale of rebates paid to film producers in proportion to the box office takings of each film. This sliding scale, when originally introduced in June 1938 by Law 106, ran from 12 per cent to 25 per cent, the percentage increasing in stages as the total takings of the film increased; thus if the producer already had plenty of butter on his bread, the state in this way gave him large

40

quantities of jam as well. But either because the absurdity of this became apparent, or simply because it cost too much, the scale was modified by Law 1131 in August 1940 so that it tapered off at the top end of the scale. In this form it ran as follows:—

			lire	*lire*	
Films grossing up to	..	.. ..		2,500,000 — 12%	rebate
,,	,,	between 2,500,000 and		4,000,000 — 15%	,,
,,	,,	,, 4,000,000 and		5,000,000 — 20%	,,
,,	,,	,, 5,000,000 and		6,000,000 — 25%	,,
,,	,,	,, 6,000,000 and		10,000,000 — 15%	,,
,,	,,	more than		10,000,000 — 12%	,,

But the fourth plank was the most ingenious of all. The Fascist State, like other dictatorships, found that their flock had an obstinate preference for the films made in that decadent Jewish pluto-democracy, America. Unlike some other dictatorships the Fascists were intelligent and flexible enough to make this perverse tendency on the part of their loyal millions into an integral part of the system. In 1938 they set up an organisation called E.N.A.I.P.E. (Ente Nazionale Importazione Pellicole Estere—National Body for Importing Foreign Films).[1] In its earlier days E.N.A.I.P.E. itself bought the films out-right from the foreign owners and then resold them to Italian distributors; it was a complete and watertight legal monopoly, for no one but E.N.A.I.P.E. was allowed to buy foreign films, and the distri-butor therefore had to buy from E.N.A.I.P.E. or not at all. But the trouble was that sometimes he did not buy at all or else he would not pay the price E.N.A.I.P.E. wanted; so the working of E.N.A.I.P.E. was considerably modified and simplified by Law 404 in April 1940 so as to leave the risk where it properly belonged—in the lap of the foreign film producer. E.N.A.I.P.E. now became simply a channel through which foreign films passed to those Italian distributors who had the right—a point explained in the following paragraph—to acquire them. E.N.A.I.P.E. was, in fact, like a shop on whose shelves are a number of packets all labelled and priced, but still the property

[1] The setting up of E.N.A.I.P.E. was an extremely rapid piece of work; indeed for once the word 'overnight' is practically justifiable, for the American and other foreign distributors were given exactly forty-eight hours in which to get out of busi-ness and leave E.N.A.I.P.E. as the only occupants of this not unprofitable field.

41

of those who made them. Thus if you were an American or other foreign producer with a film which you wished to sell in Italy you sent a print along to E.N.A.I.P.E. saying that the price was so much (the fact that most of the big distributors had been in business in Italy on their own account until very recently gave them a fairly shrewd idea of the picture's commercial value), and E.N.A.I.P.E. sold it for that figure to anyone who wanted to buy it, and who had the necessary 'buoni di doppiaggio', or dubbing coupons.

The buoni di doppiaggio system was really one of inspired simplicity. First it was made illegal to show films either in their original version or subtitled; they had to be completely dubbed into Italian, a process which enabled any necessary disinfection of the dialogue from corrupt and decadent ideas of political freedom to be carried out fairly painlessly. Secondly, films might only be dubbed by firms who possessed the necessary buoni; these were given a nominal value of 50,000 lire each; two of them were awarded to the producers of films costing between 3,000,000 and 5,000,000 and four of them to the producers of films costing over 5,000,000. The nominal value of the buoni was later raised to 75,000 lire, and the effect of distributing them to the producers of Italian films, like pennies to well-behaved children, was that the producers not only thus avoided the necessity of buying them but in fact acquired a valuable property, since the buoni were freely transferable and were often sold by producers who had no direct interest in distribution.

A minor, but not unamusing, aspect of this system was the interlocking of L.U.C.E. with another parastatal organisation called E.N.I.C. (Ente Nazionale Industrie Cinematografiche). The function of E.N.I.C. was the ownership of a chain of cinemas and film exchanges, while that of L.U.C.E. was, as already explained, the production of documentaries and of a weekly newsreel; as the L.U.C.E. newsreel was by this time the only one whose showing was permitted in Italy, and as its inclusion in every programme was compulsory, the set-up was as satisfactory, to those interested, from the financial as from the propagandist angle.

A minor but not unamusing corner of this ramshackle edifice—to change the metaphor—was the interlocking of L.U.C.E. and E.N.I.C. Of the E.N.I.C. shares 80 per cent were held by L.U.C.E. and 20 per cent by the State, so that on the face of it E.N.I.C. was controlled by L.U.C.E. and not directly by the State. But of L.U.C.E.'s own shares 40 per cent were, in turn, held by E.N.I.C. and 60 per cent by a combination of three other State-controlled organisations. These were the Assicurazione Nazionale (in effect a sort of gigantic State-controlled Friendly Society), the Cassa Infortuni (more or less Workmen's Compensation), and the Associazione Nazionale Combattenti (a State-controlled equivalent of the British Legion—or perhaps a better parallel would be the American Veterans' Administration). It will be seen that, whatever the merits of this curious system of control, clarity, simplicity and logic were not amongst them.

From at least one point of view, however, that of quantity of output (quality is always less easily disciplined), the system was not without its achievements, though the outbreak of war and consequent restriction in the flow of foreign films were a factor in the later stages. All the same, the production of Italian feature films, which had been in the region of 30 a year from 1933 to 1938, went up to 84 in 1939, 68 in 1940, 90 in 1941, and no fewer than 119 in 1942.

Chapter Five

THE YEARS BEFORE AND
DURING THE SECOND WORLD WAR

DURING 1933 there emerged quite unmistakably a certain type of sentimental comedy which was to be a conspicuous element in Italian production for some years to come. The Italians themselves, with a nice flash of wit, found the apt name for them: 'telefoni bianchi', white telephones.

Three of the better of these sentimental comedies were Guido Brignone's *Paradiso* (*Paradise*), written by Luigi Bonelli and with music by Luigi Colacicchi, Gennaro Righelli's *Al Buio Insieme* (*In the Dark Together*), written by Alessandro de Stefani and starring Maurizio d'Ancora, and Carlo L. Bragaglia's *O La Borsa O La Vita* (*Your Money Or Your Life*), also by Alessandro de Stefani but starring Sergio Tofano. This last was considerably less stage-bound than the usual run of the genre, and was distinguished by a pleasantly fantastic dream sequence which contemporary critics compared with René Clair's work. Another good example emerged, in 1934, in the shape of *Seconda B* (*Form 2B*), directed by Goffredo Alessandrini, who had just become the husband of the youthful Anna Magnani; this was one of the first films in which Maria Denis appeared—others in the cast were Sergio Tofano, Dina Perbellini, and Ugo Ceseri—and the setting, which was a school in 1912, was handled with a nicely ironic atmosphere not unreminiscent of such post-war films as Soldati's *Le Miserie de Monsu Travet* or Castellani's *Mio Figlio Professore*.

Blasetti's contribution to the year's output consisted of *La Tavola dei Poveri* and *1860*. The former was a rather mediocre vehicle for a well-known Neapolitan dialect actor, Raffaele Viviani, but the latter was a work of some sweep and importance. Taken from a story by Gino Mazzucchi it follows the adventures of a Sicilian mountaineer who leaves his newly-married wife to join Garibaldi at Genoa, and stays with him until the defeat of the Bourbon troops at Calatafimi. It contained some notably good scenes; for example, the service in the little church before the shooting, the wife's frantic search for her husband among the dead and dying of the battlefield, and her meeting with the blind soldier who believes her to be his mother so that, for a time, she is drawn to forget her husband in order to preserve the dying illusions of the mortally wounded soldier.

Two other productions of 1933 merit mention. The first is *Acciaio* (*Steel*), noteworthy because it was made by the famous German documentary director Ruttman, from a script by, oddly enough, Luigi Pirandello. The whole film was made at Terni, an industrial town a little north of Rome (rather the Italian equivalent of Corby, in Northamptonshire). The ostensible story, of which the principals were Isa Pola and Pietro Pastore, is a sufficiently banal triangle, but the film's undoubted merits derive from the excellent use that Ruttman made of his material, the scenes in the iron works, the festa scenes, the bicycle races, and so on. The second film, *Camicia Nera* (*Black Shirt*), directed by Giovacchino Forzano, is worth citing for other reasons; first, because, setting out to tell the story of a typical simple family under Fascism, it was one of the most effective of the earlier propaganda films, and secondly because Forzano anticipated a commonplace of post-war Italian production by using hardly any actors, choosing instead people who actually were what they were intended to represent on the screen.

This was followed in 1935 by Blasetti's *Vecchia Guardia* (*Old Guard*), a film made to glorify the famous 'march' on Rome when most of the Fascist legions rolled comfortably along in trucks and Mussolini himself followed by sleeping-car. Since, however, this film is far from being one of Blasetti's best, let us merely say that its making was part of the price that had to be paid in those days for permission to be a director. He was certainly much happier in the three films that followed: *Aldebaran*, in 1936, a film on the contemporary Italian Navy, and quite a good one; *La Contessa di Parma* (*The Countess of Parma*), in 1937, with Elisa Cegani, Antonio Centa, and Maria Denis, and one of the best films of his career, *Ettore Fieramosca*, in 1938. This, dealing with one of the famous Italian soldiers of fortune of the Middle Ages,

45

was in the historical vein in which Blasetti was always happiest, and the scene when Ettore Fieramosca fights the French champion in the famous 'duel of Barletta' was one highlight in a film of sweeping movement, picturesque scenes, and some fine handling of masses of men. The principal actors were Gino Cervi and Osvaldo Valenti; Blasetti himself, with three collaborators, wrote the script, and Alessandro Cicognini was responsible for the music.

This was far from being the only major historical film of the period. The old master himself, Enrico Guazzoni, made *Re Burlone* with Armando Falconi in the principal part in 1935; Guido Brignone directed *Lorenzino de Medici* the same year; and Camerini directed *Il Cappello a Tre Punte* (*The Three-Cornered Hat*); based on Alarcon's famous *Sombrero de Tres Picos*, the whole thing was light-heartedly transplanted to seventeenth-century Naples and the principal parts entrusted to those brilliant Neapolitan dialect actors, Eduardo and Peppino de Filippo.

Camerini, then rapidly developing his full powers, followed this up with a very pleasant modern comedy *Daro Un Milione* (*I'll Give a Million*), a slightly Capra-ish story of a millionaire who becomes disillusioned in the way that fictional millionaires so often do. He masquerades as a poor man, determined to give a million lire (which in those days was worth having) to the first person who shows any sign of really unselfish goodwill towards him. The story is in the episodic form natural to this sort of film, but there is a very lively invention of incident, and the feeling is very well maintained. In the cast, as well as Vittorio de Sica and Assia Noris, were Luigi Almirante who will be remembered with affection by many as the old man who played the trumpet in *Vivere in Pace*, and also appeared in *Anni Difficili* and *Campane a Martello*.[1]

About this period it became increasingly clear that the subjects suitable for film making were very closely related to those that, at any particular time, bulked large in the consciousness of the higher ranks of Fascism, and the current preoccupation with Italy's place in the African sun was reflected in a number of films with colonial subjects. Three of them were produced by Eugenio Fontana: *Lo Squadrone Bianco* (*The White Squadron*), directed by Augusto Genina in 1936; *Sentinelle di Bronzo* (*Sentinels of Bronze*), directed by Romolo Marcellini in 1937; and *Sotto La Croce del Sud* (*Under the Southern Cross*), directed

[1] Also shot simultaneously in an English version as *Children of Chance*.

by Guido Brignone in 1938. There was, too, a campaign film for the Abyssinian War in the shape of *Il Cammino degli Eroi* (*The Heroes' Journey*), a montage of some of the enormous quantity of material shot by the special camera unit under Luciano de Feo. Of all these *Lo Squadrone Bianco* was indisputably the best; it had the advantage of Fosco Giachetti in the principal part (in those days you could hardly go into a cinema without seeing Giachetti in some uniform or other on the screen, but, to do him justice, he was usually excellent and managed to portray a human being and not merely a tailor's dummy stuffed with military virtues), and the scenes of the squadron's departure, their long and arduous march across the desert, the ever-present torture of the wind and sand, and the occasional skirmishes were, odd though it may seem, very much in the same vein as Harry Watt's *Nine Men*.

Fascist propaganda, blatant though it often was in other media, seems on the screen to have been purged to a considerable degree of its grosser faults. Two of the more famous propaganda films of the period were *L'Assedio dell' Alcazar* (*The Siege of Alcazar*) (1940), and *Bengasi* (1942), both of them directed by Genina and produced by Bassoli. The former was made immediately after the end of the Spanish Civil War, in which Italian intervention had by that time been more or less officially acknowledged. And though the Republican soldiers have perhaps a rather conspicuous tendency to be unshaven and to smoke cigarettes on duty, the character of the commanding officer on the—to the Italians—enemy side was presented with considerable sympathy and humanity. Though there is naturally no attempt to present an impartial survey of the causes or conduct of that bloodiest of civil wars, one is bound to admit that the blacks are much less black than in most of the British or American films with which one could reasonably compare it.

The production of *Bengasi*, which was made in 1942, followed a rather chequered course, for it was made during the time when the campaign was actually being fought; it will be remembered that Benghazi, to give it its English spelling, changed hands several times during the fighting. Whenever it happened to be in our possession work on the film was promptly stopped, for commercial as well as political reasons, only to be pressed rapidly forward whenever the Italians regained possession of the town. In spite of this rather syncopated history the finished film was quite a first class piece of work, and if the British in it are not exactly the picture of honour, they are certainly no worse than the average Italian or German in the films we made during the war, and considerably better than many.

But the major effort of the Italian film industry in the immediately pre-war years was *Scipione l' Africano* (1937) which was intended to remind the latter-day Italians of the glories of their past in the period of Imperial Rome, and, once again, to repeat the theme of the African empire. The screen play was written by Carmine Gallone, Camillo Mariani dell' Anguillara, and S. A. Luciani, with sets and costumes by Pietro Aschieri and an elaborate musical score by Ildebrando Pizzetti. It was directed by Carmine Gallone, and the demands of the production in the way of financial and material resources were so great that a special combine, consisting of all the largest producing houses, was formed to carry this responsibility. In spite of Gallone's competence as a director, and in spite of the presence in the cast of such popular stars as Fosco Giachetti, Isa Miranda and Annibale Ninchi, the whole thing sagged very badly, and people spoke with malicious pleasure of such incongruities as the telegraph poles which could be seen in the background of a Punic battle and the wrist-watches on the arms of the extras playing in the Roman crowd. Perhaps the truth is that these enormous grandiose historical spectacles are only tolerable when they are carried along by the genius of a Griffith or a Guazzoni or at least a Blasetti; perhaps, too, it is necessary that the film should be made, as those classical examples *Birth of a Nation, Intolerance*, and *Quo Vadis?* were made—because one man's implacable determination was the moving force behind the whole enterprise so that the very obstacles that he encounters serve only as temporary dams behind which fresh force piles up. It may not be too fanciful to say that an epic film must be made in something of the same spirit as an epic poem is written; and it is quite certain that no one ever wrote a *Paradise Lost* or a *Divina Commedia* because he was assigned to it.

The founding in 1935 of the Direzione Generale per la Cinematografia was recorded in Chapter Four; two other developments that marked the increasing governmental interest in the cinema were the founding, later in the same year, of the Centro Sperimentale della Cinematografia and the taking over of Cinecitta. The Centro Sperimentale was, and probably still is, an institution with no parallel outside Russia. Conducted since its foundation by Luigi Chiarini, who is still its head, it sets out to teach people who hope to work on the creative side of

48

QUO VADIS?

QUO VADIS?

QUO VADIS?
1913
Enrico Guazzoni

CABIRIA
1914
Giovanni Pastrone

MESSALINA

MESSALINA

MESSALINA
1924
Enrico Guazzoni

PINA MENICHELLI
Star of the early Italian cinema

I TOPI GRIGI

I TOPI GRIGI
1917
Emilio Ghione

SPERDUTI NEL BUIO
1914
Nino Martoglio

LA CANZONE DELL'AMORE
1930
Gennaro Righelli

IL CANALE DEGLI ANGELI
1934
P. M. and F. Pasinetti

PICCOLO MONDO ANTICO
1941
Mario Soldati

DANIELE CORTIS
1947
Mario Soldati

LE MISERIE DEL SIG. TRAVET
1945
Mario Soldati

UN COLPO DI PISTOLA
1942
Renato Castellani

I CONDOTTIERI
1937
Luis Trenker

LA DONNA DELLA MONTAGNA
1943
Renato Castellani

SCIPIONE L'AFRICANO
1937
Carmine Gallone

1860
1933
Alessandro Blasetti

ETTORE FIERAMOSCA
1938
Alessandro Blasetti

FABIOLA

FABIOLA

FABIOLA
1948
Alessandro Blasetti

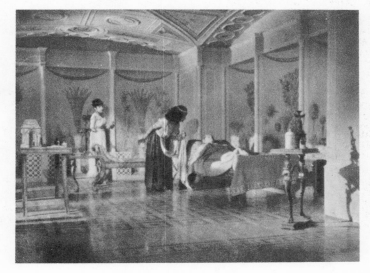

L'ASSEDIO DELL'ALCAZAR
1940
Augusto Genina

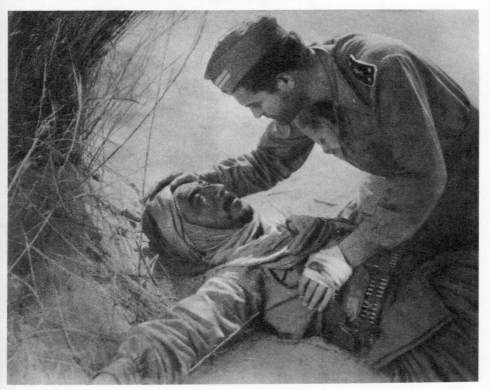

SQUADRONE BIAN
1938
Augusto Genina

HARLEM
1943
Carmine Gallone

BENGASI
1942
Augusto Genina

ACCIAIO (STEEL)

ACCIAIO (STEEL)
1933
Walther Ruttmann

COMACCHIO
1942
Fernando Cerchio

LE ISOLE DELLA LAGUNA
1948
Luciano Emmer and Enrico Gras

I ROMANTICI A VENEZIA
1948
Luciano Emmer and Enrico Gras

IL PIANTO DELLE ZITELLE
1940
Giacomo Pozzi Bellini

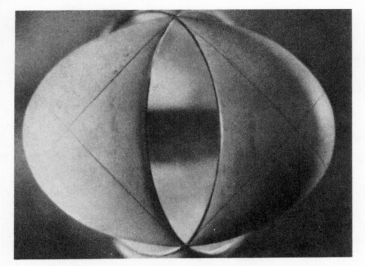

UNA LEZIONE IN GEOMETRIA
1948
Leonardo Sinisgalli

PIAZZA SAN MARCO

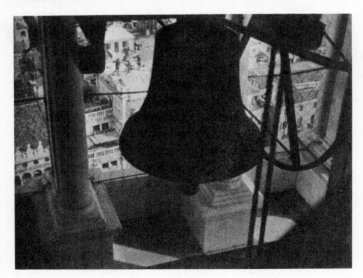

PIAZZA SAN MARCO
1947
Francesco Pasinetti

SULLA VIA DI DAMASCO
1947
Luciano Emmer and Enrico Gras

IL DRAMMA DI CRISTO
(Giotto Frescoes)
1940; remade 1948
Luciano Emmer

IL GIORNO DELLA SALUTE
1948
Francesco Pasinetti

OSSESSIONE

OSSESSIONE

OSSESSIONE
1942
Luchino Visconti

OSSESSIONE

OSSESSIONE

OSSESSIONE
1942
Luchino Visconti

IL BANDITO

IL BANDITO
1946
Alberto Lattuada

SCIUSCIÀ (SHOESHINE)
1946
Vittorio de Sica

UN AMERICANO
IN VACANZA

UN AMERICANO
IN VACANZA
1945
Luigi Zampa

GIOVENTÙ PERDUTA
1947
Pietro Germi

FIGLIO PROFESSORE
1946
Renato Castellani

SENZA PIETÀ
1947
Alberto Lattuada

COME PERSI LA GUERRA
1947
Carlo Borghesio

SOTTO IL SOLE DI ROMA
1948
Renato Castellani

L'ONOREVOLE ANGELINA
1947
Luigi Zampa

FUGA IN FRANCIA
1948
Mario Soldati

ANNI DIFFICILI
1948
Luigi Zampa

LA TERRA TREMA
(Episodio del Mare)
1948
Luchino Visconti

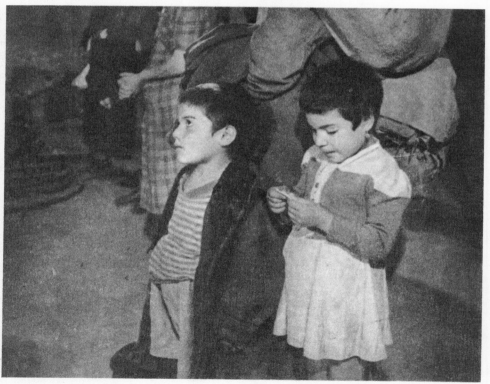

LADRI DI
BICICLETTE
1948
Vittorio de Sica

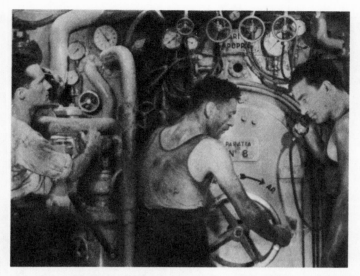

UOMINI SUL FONDO
1940
Francesco de Robertis

MARINAI SENZA STELLE
1943
Francesco de Robertis

LA VITA SEMPLICE
1945
Francesco de Robertis

ROMA CITTÀ APERTA

ROMA CITTÀ APERTA

ROMA CITTÀ APERTA
(ROME OPEN CITY)
1945
Roberto Rossellini

ROMA CITTÀ APERTA
(ROME OPEN CITY)
1945
Roberto Rossellini

PAISÀ
The Sicilian Episode

PAISÀ
The Neapolitan Episode
1946
Roberto Rossellini

PAISÀ
The Episode in Rome

PAISÀ
The Episode in Florence

PAISÀ
The Episode in the Monastery
1946
Roberto Rossellini

PAISÀ
The Episode in the Po Marshlands   1946   Roberto Rossellini

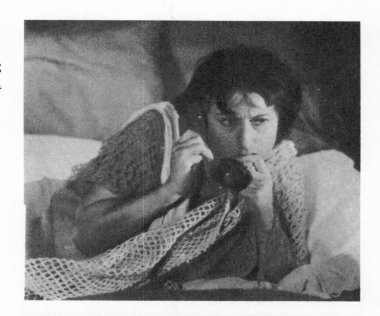

AMORE
Part I—La Voce Umana

AMORE
Part II—The Miracle
1948
Roberto Rossellini

GERMANIA, ANNO ZERO

GERMANIA, ANNO ZERO
1947
Roberto Rossellini

LA MACCHINA AMMAZZACATTIVI
1948
Roberto Rossellini

production everything relevant that can be taught in a college; acting, direction, set design, costume design, cutting and editing, the writing of scenarios are all tackled in the two years that the course lasts, with the result that, in whatever branch of the industry the student eventually settles down, he is likely to have a much more balanced idea about what the other people are doing than might be the case with a technician who has worked his way up from a clapper boy to the director's chair. Two aspects of the Centro are of especial value; the first is that Chiarini is himself a very competent director with quite a reasonable list of successes to his credit, while his present assistant, Pasinetti,[1] is one of the best documentary directors now working in Italy; this, and the presence of many practising designers, writers, and others at the Centro removes any taint of inappropriate academicism; another admirable aspect is that the Centro possesses two first-class stages, where commercial films are often made, and where it is often possible to allow students to work on normal productions under normal conditions; for example, the master designs for a set may be made by the man responsible for the architecture of the film, but the detailed drawings may be made, under his supervision, by the students. And the roll of present-day star Italian producers, directors, actors and actresses, writers and designers who have graduated from the Centro is a proof of the excellence of its work.

Cinecitta, probably the largest studios in Europe, were opened in 1937. They owed their existence entirely to the enormous enthusiasm and drive of Carlo Roncoroni, and it was one of the tragedies of the Italian film industry that he should have died tragically only a few months after the great studios were finally ready for shooting. With their sixteen stages, their 600,000 sq. metres of ground, their long corridors of dressing-rooms, and their quite uncharacteristic (for the cinema) air of spaciousness, they were the showpiece of the Italian cinema. After Roncoroni's death the Government took over the studios and ran them directly, and the bulk of Italian production during war-time and in the immediately pre-war years took place there. Damaged by Allied bombing and shelling, looted of all movable machinery by the retreating Germans, first a prisoner of war camp and then a centre for displaced persons, they were in a sorry state down to the end of 1947 when the Government entrusted Tito Marconi with the task of getting them back into working order. He succeeded well enough for

[1] Pasinetti, who was under forty, died suddenly in the summer of 1949.

49

Twentieth Century Fox to complete all the studio work for *Prince of Foxes* there; as well as for Universalia to do much of the production of *Fabiola* and *Gli Ultimi Giorni* there. But this is getting rather ahead of our story.

The fantastic financial structure which the Fascist government set up in the film industry was described in some detail in Chapter Four. The result of this combination of subsidies, rebates, provision of capital and secured markets made film production a gold mine. A producer could initiate the production of a film without having a lira of his own, and when it was finished he could be sure that he would get back its cost and very probably a useful profit into the bargain.

Naturally enough those who formed the fortunate circle were anxious not to admit newcomers; equally naturally all the "good Fascists" suddenly developed a passionate interest in film production, led by Mussolini's son Vittorio, who founded a house for the production and distribution of films under the name of Europa. One of the bright particular stars of Europa was Myria di San Servolo, the sister of the Duce's mistress Clara Petacci. Myria di San Servolo made only two films; considering their conspicuous lack of success that was probably all for the best, especially for Europa. Another of Europa's discoveries was Michela Belmonte; she, too, made only two films—two seems to have been Vittorio Mussolini's lucky number—and one of them was *I Tre Aquilotti* (*The Three Eaglets*) (1942), a film on which Rossellini tried his then prentice hand though it is now, by tacit consent, tactfully omitted from the canon of his works.

In their endeavour to maintain the principle of the closed shop the producing and distributing houses had succeeded in promoting legislation that limited their number to eighteen. There were already eighteen in existence before Europa made its sudden appearance, and Europa was followed by two others in whose cases any contraceptive tactics would have been equally ill-advised. But by a miracle of Fascist arithmetic the number remained fixed at eighteen. The cutting up of the joint into eighteen slices with which to satisfy twenty-one voracious appetites must have been a pretty sight for those with a taste for irony.

The virtual elimination of foreign competition, the protected market, and the irruption into the industry of rank and self-important amateurs, had the effect one would expect. The standards of production began to fall, and the majority of films consisted of shallow comedies shot with only two or three changes of scene. The miracle is that so many producers and directors did retain some sense of professional pride and responsibility. Some, like Soldati, made only historical films, the alternatives of propaganda glorifying the regime or white-telephone films being equally unacceptable to them. When Bassoli and Genina made *L'Assedio dell' Alcazar* they spent seven and a half million lire on it; the other producers, or many of them, looked at them in honest bewilderment. The idea that Bassoli and Genina were making the film as well as they possibly could was outside the range of their comprehension.

One or two films of the period are, however, worth at least recording. One of the better propaganda films was *Luciano Serra Pilota* (1938), directed by Goffredo Alessandrini and 'supervised' by Vittorio Mussolini. No fewer than five people, including Rossellini, helped Alessandrini to write the screen play, and the photography was by Arata, the cameraman of *Open City*; the basic theme of the story was the instinctive passion for flying that descends from father to son, with the climax of the film coming when the father heroically loses his own life during the Abyssinian war to save that of his son. Rossellini's early *Un Pilota Ritorna* (*A Pilot Returns*) (1942) is not without merit, though it bears no comparison with his post-war work. Another film that had some quite outstanding merits was *Un Colpo di Pistola* (*A Pistol Shot*) (1942), directed by Castellani. This was one of the earliest films of the man who was later to make *Mio Figlio Professore* and *Sotto il Sole di Roma*. A rather romantic film in something of the same vein as Soldati's *Piccolo Mondo Antico* and set in the early nineteenth century, it was very widely praised for the perfection of its detail, and for camera work which was beautifully mannered without ever verging on the precious. Blasetti, working in a field strange to him, that of sentimental comedy, directed in *Quattro Passi fra le Nuvole* (*A Stroll in the Clouds*) the only pre-war Italian film so far to have had any success, post-war, in England. Beautifully acted by Adriana Benetti and Gino Cervi, the film is too well known in England to need any further description. Much more in Blasetti's usual vein, and a really outstanding film, was his *La Cena delle Beffe* (*The Supper of Hoaxes*) (1941), with a cast that included Osvaldo Valenti, Amedeo Nazzari, Clara Calamai, Valentina Cortese and Luisa Ferida. Based on a famous play of fourteenth-century Florence, this is historical drama at its best with its involved intrigues, riotous passions, bloody revenges, elaborate hoaxes and all the glittering panoply of an age considerably more dramatic and extravert than our own. Minstrels, singing their traditional songs; night watchmen calling the hours; the story-tellers with their much-repeated but ever-welcome tales; the criers bringing the citizens the news of the day—all these and hundreds more of the picturesque aspects of the period throng the screen, and the handling of the principal scenes was extraordinarily good; such scenes as that in which Amadeo Nazzari is hunted up and down the great bell tower, or the great supper scene itself, or that in which Osvaldo Valenti, knowing that Nazzari's return will mean his death, still waits for the inevitable, held motionless by his overwhelming sense of guilt.

With the signing of the armistice on September 8th, 1943, the whole of the cinema world, like most other Italian worlds at that moment, fell into two sharply divided parties. In one were to be found those who were either secret sympathisers of the Allies or who simply felt that the Axis was the losing side with which they did not wish to be compromised; in the other were those who out of sympathy or loyalty or plain miscalculation, remained attached to the Fascist Republicans when they set up the Republic of Saló. Those who formed the first party went into various forms of discreet hiding until a suitable moment for re-emergence should present itself; the latter moved up to Venice, where production was concentrated in Scalera's Venetian studios for the few remaining months. With those directors, producers and technicians who went north went also some of the better-known actors and actresses, amongst them two of the leading stars of the period, Osvaldo Valenti and Luisa Ferida. For some time there had been a great deal of very ugly gossip about their private lives, and in the chaotic period about the end of the Italian campaign this reached new heights; it was widely reported that they had been indulging in sadistic orgies at the expense of the Fascists' prisoners, and though it is now impossible to decide whether these stories were true or not, they were so well believed that the Partisans shot them out of hand when they caught up with them at the villa which was the reputed scene of their crimes of violence.

So closed the scene of the pre-war Italian cinema, in an atmosphere of violence, confusion and corruption that was characteristic of most of the aspects of Italian life that had been either developed or taken over by the Fascists. But before we leave this period some little time must be spared for a most astonishing single swallow whose summer was not to follow until the post-war renaissance was in full flower. This odd and

52

early harbinger, quite the most astonishing and unlikely film to emerge from a Fascist-dominated industry, was Luchino Visconti's *Ossessione* (*Obsession*) (1942).

Not the least astonishing thing about this film is that it was Visconti's first film; it is true that he had for some years been working in France under Renoir, but this was his first solo flight, and in it he certainly showed that those years had not been wasted. This is a film which, writing in all sobriety after having seen it several times, cannot be called less than a masterpiece, so flawless is it in its conception and presentation of character, so admirably controlled in its narration, and so consistent in its atmosphere.

Copyright is so controversial a subject that it is better not to write more than that the story of *Ossessione* has certain affinities with James Cain's *The Postman Always Rings Twice*. The setting of the Italian story, however, is not the Pacific coast of Cain's story any more than the characters are his Greek-American and American silhouettes; Visconti's background is the flat marshy country where the Po begins to widen out into its delta and it is here that, in a rough wayside trattoria, or inn, he had brought his characters to life with astonishing skill.

The husband is middle-aged, fat, greasy, kindly, uxorious, completely normal for his world. The wife is a passionate slut, an Italian Madame Bovary, with more of the flesh and less of the sentiment, moved by something more than lust and less than love, something that takes possession of her, uses her, and throws her away when it has done with her, a woman with something of the temperament of a Borgia but lacking the will or ability to overcome the handicaps of her lack of education and breeding. The lover is a much more ordinary character than the wife, not so much frightened as uneasy, embarrassed at having raised unwittingly a storm which he can neither match nor ride: you understand him perfectly when you see him seeking refuge in the arms of a cheap little trollop whom he picks up on one of his attempts to escape from his fate, because here he has something with which he can cope.

Visconti has placed these characters in a setting of the most convincing reality. Realism may not be by any means an essential artistic virtue but in this type of film it is a necessity, for without it everything falls to the ground. The trattoria itself, the surrounding countryside, the railway trains, the fair at Ancona, the day-long crowds at the trattoria when there is a festa, the host of minor characters, the crowds, all are superlatively real. You can almost smell the garlic and the sweat, taste the harsh red wine and the bowls of minestrone, feel the hot sun on your face and the gritty road underneath your feet.

The part of the husband is played by Juan de Landa, a minor actor who here found his one perfect part and was induced (or allowed) to play it perfectly. The wife is played by Clara Calamai, an actress of distinction who has always done her best work in parts of this sort but has never before or since equalled her work in *Ossessione*. Massimo Girotti plays the lover, and to write that he plays it with complete adequacy sounds like faint praise; actually it is high praise, for a part of this sort, where most of the sympathy and most of the drama belong to the other two, is difficult indeed. Against the sultry devouring passion of the wife he can offer only a sudden flame of simple desire which dies as suddenly down again; he must portray an increasing uneasiness which is more instinctive than understood, like that of an animal that scents the abattoir; he must show satiety and fear and distaste as, after the husband's murder, he finds himself saddled with a woman he does not want.

To our three principals Visconti added an extra character, a wandering cheap-jack and vagabond played with the same superb realism as the others by Elio Marcuzzo. His addition was a minor inspiration. The lover meets him when he has fled from the trattoria, from the husband of whom he has become jealous, from the wife whose uncontrolled passion is beginning to frighten him. Elio Marcuzzo embodies for him the visible ideal of his old life, the life of carefree vagabondage, and its juxtaposition adds the final ironic touch to his bitterness and his destruction when he finds that his unwilling involvement in an intrigue that oppresses and distresses him has also made it impossible for him to go back to his life of wandering irresponsibility.

Let us consider one or two of the episodes which Visconti has so beautifully contrived. There has been a festa at the trattoria. All day the place has been crowded with the people from the surrounding countryside—dancing, drinking, eating, sweating, playing at bocce, a simple, animal, peasant holiday. Now they have all gone and the woman and her lover are alone, with only the memory of the murdered husband between them. The lover has gone upstairs to bed alone, resentful, trapped, seeking to drown his fears and angers in drink. The woman is left alone. She wanders out into the kitchen which is piled high with the debris of the day's business—dirty glasses, empty bottles, odds and ends of food, stacks of plates. Taking a plate she slops a little soup into it and sits down at the corner of the table with the plate in her lap, obviously so weary that she can hardly find the energy to swallow. Into the little circle of lamplight in the middle of the squalid confusion in which she sits she pulls an old newspaper and sits on, so tired that she can hardly move her jaws to eat, or understand what she is reading. Finally she puts down the half-eaten soup and, pushing it away, lets her head sink on to her arms on a corner of the littered kitchen table, more collapsed than sleeping, while upstairs her lover is probably snoring in a drunken sleep. This, you realise, is the wages of sin. This is not only the end to which their actions have brought them, it is the end which was implicit in their beginning. There is no hint of moral judgement; there is just an inevitability that has its own form of beauty.

Or consider the passage leading up to the husband's murder. He and his wife have gone to Ancona for a festa, and there they meet the lover who, shortly before, had left them when he failed to persuade the wife to run away with him. The inn-keeper, who has a sneaking affection for the young man and who, secure in his prosperity and married state, likes to patronise him, carries him off with them to the café where he is going to take part in a singing competition. The efforts of the competitors, including the inn-keeper, are treated with a nicely mordant humour; they are ordinary, silly, even ridiculous people, observed with understanding and accuracy and presented without any merciful softening; the audience are ordinary, pleasant, vulgar, commonplace people. And in the midst of all this, devoured by their lust, and as incongruous as a couple of tigers in a farmyard, sit the wife and her lover. The contrast and the tension are really frightening.

The inn-keeper wins the contest, and is treated to drinks by everybody, and you next see the three on their way to the garage where the truck has been left, the husband staggering and lurching and singing and belching, the other two withdrawn in their miasma of hate and desire. On the way home the husband's stomach begins to rebel against the quantity of wine he has drunk. He stops the car, stumbles out of the cab, and sits down on a kilometre stone in the light of the headlamp. Presently he turns away from the light and as the camera switches back to the lovers in the cab of the truck you hear the unmistakable sounds of the husband retching. This is not just crude and unnecessary

55

realism. It is the catalyst. It provides the necessary spring to action. It is the final and irrefutable proof of the impossibility, for the wife, of continuing to live with her fat, elderly and repulsive husband; for the lover, of allowing this mass of sodden flesh to possess the woman that he cannot have. You realise, with a sudden flash of blinding insight, that in vomiting the husband signed his own death warrant.

Chapter Six

THE POST-WAR RENAISSANCE—PART ONE

THE post-war renaissance of the Italian film began with the production of *Roma Citta Aperta* (*Rome—Open City*) in 1944; this was not only the first film actually made in liberated Italy, the first Italian film since silent days to have any real success outside Italy, and the first film to indicate the great potential talents of Roberto Rossellini; it was also the film which, because of its innate force and conviction even more than because of its success, set the tone for serious production for some years to follow.

Roma Citta Aperta was really born in Maria Michi's little flat in Via Giulio Bechi in Rome. During the German occupation of Rome, Maria Michi, who plays the drug-taking cabaret-dancer girl friend of a resistance leader, was one of those largely unsung but invaluable elements in the resistance movement, the cross between a letter-box and a one-night doss-house without which the whole thing would have broken down. It was in the drains of her flat that copies of *Unita* and *Avanti* were hidden in the awkward interval between printing and distribution; it was on the sofa in her sitting-room, which you see slightly glamorised and enlarged in the film, that such men as Togliatti, Celeste Negarville (war-time resistance leader and post-war Communist Mayor of Turin) and Sergio Amidei slept when caution counselled an absence from their better-known haunts; and it was here that, in long conversations after the early curfew, was born the idea of a film that should record this time, its dangers, its heroisms, its humours and its humanities.

The film was made under the greatest difficulties, both financial and technical. It was started with the backing of a certain Countess who had only 4,000,000 lire (about £10,000) available in cash in Rome, but who hoped to be able to get more money from Milan by the time it was needed. Her estimates of the speed of the Allied advance were, like those of many more expert than her, over-optimistic and the money came to an end long before the Allies got to Milan. She then tried to raise money on her most treasured possession, a reputed Mantegna, only to find that the picture was a fake. Rossellini and the others who were interested scraped together odd sums of money, but the film was frequently interrupted simply because there was no money to carry on, and Rossellini spent almost more time looking for money than in directing the film. Not a single producing or distributing house in Rome was willing to take a chance, and it is on record that on one occasion both Rossellini and Magnani sold all their clothes to have enough money to carry on for a few more days, while the cast worked without pay and even, like Maria Michi, lent their furniture because there was no money to hire furniture. Finally an angel in the shape of a Sig. Venturini, a Florentine silk merchant, came up with the 12,000,000 lire necessary to finish the film.

The technical difficulties were even greater. There was no proper negative and in fact the whole film was shot on odds and ends of raw-stock, bits twenty metres, fifty metres, a hundred and fifty metres long, of all sorts of mixed makes—old Ferrania, older Ferrania, Kodak, Agfa, Gaevert, and some that was quite anonymous. The supply of electricity was not only frequently lacking altogether but fluctuated from minute to minute so violently that you could see it with the naked eye, the voltage dropping by as much as fifteen or twenty volts, the frequency from fifty to forty or even lower. It is little short of marvellous that in these circumstances Ubaldo Arata, that much-loved and much-lamented cameraman (he died in 1947) was able to turn out so quietly competent a piece of work.

Nearly all the scenes were shot on the actual locations which they represent in the film. The only exceptions were the Gestapo head-quarters (a studio reconstruction of the infamous house in the Via Tasso), Don Pietro's room, and Marina's flat, which is a studio recon-struction of Maria Michi's flat, enlarged enough to be practicable; you could not even get a camera in the original, let alone lights and half a dozen technicians. These few sets were built in Capitani's tiny studio in the Via degli Avignonesi, a one-stage studio measuring about sixty feet by twenty.

This method of working was partly due to the necessity for economy, but even without that necessity Rossellini would have worked in the same way, as he has done since when money was more plentiful. Like many other Italian directors, he feels that the host of little difficulties and problems that arise when a director works in this way are more than balanced by the extra sense of reality that can be obtained. If confirmation of the validity of this fact were wanted it could be found in such American films as *Boomerang, Call Northside 777* or *The Naked City*, in which the atmosphere is subtly but strikingly different from that of the most careful studio reconstruction.

It is, too, at least possible that this method of working is particularly important when, like Rossellini, you work largely and for preference with people who are not professional actors. Most documentary directors from Flaherty to Eisenstein have shown that you can get the most superbly natural results from people who have never seen a motion-picture camera before provided that they are doing the things which they are used to do in the places where they are used to doing them. For an example we can take the performance in the opening sequence by the two old ladies when the Germans come searching for Manfredi; these two women were, in fact, Sergio Amidei's landladies, and it was in his flat that the sequence was shot.

The conception of the characters was informed by the same realisms as the choice of locations. The part of Don Pietro, the priest, played by Aldo Fabrizi, is for example a composite portrait of two priests, Don Morosini and Don Papagallo, both of whom were executed by the Germans for their work in aiding resistance leaders and escaped Allied prisoners; Manfredi, the resistance leader, is largely based on the experiences of Celeste Negarville; Pina, the part of his betrothed (played by Anna Magnani), was taken from that of a woman who was shot by the Germans in the Via Giulio Cesare, in exactly the way seen in the film, when she was inciting the women of a popular quarter to throw stones at the men who had taken her husband away; even the sadistic and perverted Gestapo chief, played by Harry Feist, is a composite portrait of Kapler, the infamous boss of the dreaded Gestapo head-quarters in the Via Tasso, and Dolman, German commander of Rome during the occupation.

Roma Citta Aperta sets out to do one thing only—to recapture as faithfully as possible the atmosphere and incidents of Rome during the German occupation, with a special but not exclusive emphasis on the work of the Resistance and of those associated with them. From its

59

first frame, its first bar of music, it sets the key unerringly. Consider the first two sequences: the very opening of the film, when the Red Cross truck, seen from high up (a fugitive's-eye-view) in one of the near-by houses, draws up in the Piazza and the German soldiery pour out and come thumping through the flat in search of Manfredi; and the second sequence, when we are in the broad light of day among the undisciplined, thrusting mob of women, jostling round the bakery in the hope of getting some of the inadequate bread ration.

Not only are these the two keynotes of the Rome of that period—danger and excitement for those active in the Resistance, worry and petty preoccupations for those attempting to lead ordinary lives—but each in turn is lighted by a counter-play of other elements. In the search sequence there is the comedy of the two old ladies alone in the flat, their fears and fumbling attempts to disarm the suspicions of the Germans; in the breadshop episode there is the broad yet pathetic comedy of the policeman who accompanies Pina home, helping to carry her hardly-won bag of bread and shamefacedly accepting the two rolls which were the purpose of the exercise—accepting them because he needs them for his family.

This balance of tragic against comic, so characteristic of life and so rare on the screen, runs through the whole film, and it would be easy to indicate a hundred examples. In the middle of the tragic and brutal sequence when the Germans and the Fascists search the tenement block in the Prenestino district of Rome where Manfredi and his comrade have been hiding, there is the beautiful little episode as Don Pietro hides the machine-gun in the bed of the invalid, knocking him unconscious with a frying-pan when he protests. But you never see the invalid hit; all you see is the boy Marcello, the priest's server, picking up the pan, looking ruefully at the dent and then at the unconscious grandfather, and saying 'Ammappelo, Don Pietro, che padellata!' an almost untranslatable Roman dialect pun meaning roughly "He's been properly panned'.

For another example there is the band of little boys who, living in the same tenement under the leadership of their one-legged boy chief, have just blown up a German dump—an episode based on real life. They come scampering back to the tenement after the explosion and as they race up the staircase each in turn, as he passes his door, is snatched inside by his parents, no longer a hero of the Resistance but just a little boy who has been out later than he should and who is afraid, not of

60

death or the Germans, but of getting his father's strap or the back of his mother's hand.

Another of the manifold excellencies of the film is the music, composed, like the music for all Rossellini's films, by his brother Renzo Rossellini. This has been strangely ignored by the critics, which is perhaps a tribute to the magnificently unobtrusive way in which it does its work. Renzo Rossellini has indeed been very sparing in his use of music, and rightly so in a film which shows actuality of the most bare and bitter kind. There is the harsh and martial musical theme which heralds the approach of the Germans; and there is the beautiful, haunting, elegiac theme used to symbolise the tenement children who are themselves a tragic little element in the Resistance, a theme which, by its incarnation of childishness, underlines the tragic disharmony between the simplicity of their youth and the horror of the actions that surround and pervade it. Apart from these two themes music is hardly used at all in the film, except for a few bars at moments such as that of the rescue of the men from the German trucks taking them away from the tenement, where it is used to heighten the excitement. With admirable restraint—which Hollywood and Elstree might copy—no music at all is used during long sequences, such as that of the searching of the tenement block, or the preparations, at the end of the film, for Don Pietro's execution.

Roma Citta Aperta won most of its fame, perhaps in Italy and certainly abroad, by the outspokenness of its realism, and the extraordinary convincingness of its torture scenes; these, indeed, are so real that it is not unusual for people to be overcome by them. But many a quite unworthy gangster film has had these qualities in almost the same degree; the great quality that shines out from the whole film is its humanity. Its characters are realised in the round, to borrow E. M. Forster's phrase, with such extraordinary completeness. Manfredi, a hero of the Resistance, but heroic only in his death; as a character an ordinary all-too-human man, frequently doubtful, tired, or irritable, almost absent-minded in his affection for Pina; Pina, with her overtones of virago and slut that only half mask her great heart: Marina, as much in love as her meretricious little heart will allow, and betraying in the end not out of treachery but out of weakness: Don Pietro, frightened all the time, and yet giving courage to others . . . the list is endless for there is not a character that does not seem to have been completely realised.

61

They used to say of Duse that once, musing about a part, she mentioned some incident and then added 'But of course that was years before she married''. The play starts with the character's marriage, but Duse had imagined for her a complete life that began before the play and went on after it. The parallel is quite apt; for every character in *Roma Citta Aperta* seems to be a person with a complete life of which the part you see in the film is only a brief extract and it is difficult to imagine a greater tribute to the quality of Rossellini's imagination or of the performances he got from his cast.

An early paragraph in this chapter said that *Roma Citta Aperta* set the tone for serious Italian production for some years to follow. If this seems an overstatement, if it seems only an accident that *Roma Citta Aperta* happened to be the first to get itself made, that it was just the crest of a wave and not the cause of the wave, then consider the other films made in the same year, 1944. Here is the complete list. Not only is every film in the list almost entirely unknown outside Italy, but the titles in most cases speak for themselves all too clearly.

L' Innocente Casimiro	*Casimir the Innocent.*
Il Processo delle Zitelle	*The Trial of the Old Maids.*
Lo Sbaglio di Essere Vivo	*The Mistake of Being Alive.*
Il Mondo Vuole Cosi ..	*This is How the World Wants It.*
Malia	*The Enchantment.*
La Freccia nel Fianco	*The Arrow in the Side.*
Le Due Modelle	*The Two Models.*
Due Lettere Anonime ..	*Two Anonymous Letters.*
Che Distinta Famiglia	*What a Distinguished Family.*
I Dieci Commandamenti	*The Ten Commandments.*
Desiderio ..	*Desire.*
L'Angelo e Il Diavolo	*The Angel and the Devil.*
Il Ratto delle Sabine ..	*The Rape of the Sabines.*
Quartetto Pazzo	*A Mad Quartet.*
Scadenza Giorni 30	*Due in 30 Days.*
Ritorno al Nido	*Return to the Nest.*

The other films that are deservedly prominent in Italian post-war production come later; in most cases much later. *Sciuscia* (*Shoeshine*) was made in 1945; *Il Bandito* (*The Bandit*), and *Un Giorno nella Vita* (*One Day of Life*) in 1946, *Vivere in Pace* (*Living in Peace*), *Caccia*

Tragica (*Tragic Hunt*), and *L'Onorevole Angelina* (*Angelina M.P.*) in 1947; *Sotto Il Sole di Roma* (*Under the Roman Sun*), *Anni Difficili* (*The Difficult Years*), and *Ladri di Biciclette* (*Bicycle Thieves*) in 1948.

If, then, we grant that Rossellini's influence, direct and indirect, was outstanding, it may be interesting to depart from a chronological study of Italian cinema as a whole to examine his subsequent films on their own. In 1945–46 he made *Paisa*—the title is untranslatable: it was the American soldiers' affectionate-contemptuous name for any Italian; in 1947 *Germania Anno Zero* (*Germany Year Nought*); in 1947–48 *Amore* (*Love*), in 1948 *La Macchina Amazzacattivi* (*The Camera that Kills the Wicked*), and in 1949 *Stromboli*.

Paisa is a series of unconnected episodes, unconnected, that is, except in emotional tension and rhythm, designed to illustrate the progress of the war in its slow drag up the length of Italy. The basic plan is probably one that sounds better than it works out in practice, for the lack of continuity prevents the audience developing that measure of imaginative identification with the characters on the screen which is so important a part in the success of a dramatic film. The ordinary film-goer is apt to feel much the same dissatisfaction as the average lending library customer professes to suffer from a volume of short stories.

The first episode shows an American patrol in Sicily (the sequence was actually shot at Majori a little south of Ravello in the Sorrento peninsula) guided by a Sicilian girl who is subsequently shot by the Germans and wrongly believed by the Americans to have been a traitor. The episode catches something of the confused aimlessness and uncertainty typical of infantry fighting, but is poorish largely because Rossellini's inveterate habit of shooting off the cuff left him short of material when he came to edit this episode. The second is a considerable improvement. A drunken Negro military policeman on a spree is appropriated by one of those incredible Neapolitan scugnizzi (the Naples variety of dead-end kids) who, after listening to the Negro's drunken raving about the glories of New York, steals his boots and leaves him. A day or so later, clean, sober and spruced up, the Negro finds the urchin again and, threatening him with dire penalties, sets off with him in search of his stolen boots, following him until they end up in the vast caverns where at that time thousands of Neapolitans were living like animals, a scene from which he turns away in terror, horror and shame.

63

In the third episode an American soldier, played by Gar Moore, returns to Rome on leave, six months after the Allies' entry, to look for the girl he met that dusty, hot, flower-laden and cheer-filled day when he brought his liberating tank through the streets of Rome. He meets her; but in the intervening six months she has become a prostitute, and he is too drunk to recognise her, too drunk even to make love. All he can do is maunder about the girl he remembers, and lament that all the girls go the same way. She leaves him asleep, and gives the landlady the address of her old room, where she goes to wait for him the following morning. But when another soldier asks him what the slip of paper is he replies 'Just another whore's address', crumples it up, and throws it away unread. Maria Michi's acting as the prostitute is simple and moving, and the episode reveals the inevitable degradation, the spoiling of good and simple things, that follows like a disease in the wake of an army. The only criticism one can make is that the situation in which the man and woman find each other again is like a novelette, a little too neat; perhaps for once in his life Rossellini made a compromise.

The fourth episode shows Harriet White as an American nurse looking for her resistance-leader sweetheart in the bullet-swept streets of Florence during that odd interregnum when the Allies held the south bank of the Arno and the Germans the north, harassed by the Partisans fighting in their midst. It is memorable mainly for a brilliant thumbnail sketch of two British officers in an observation post, not exactly cynical but sharper than humour, and revealing a facet of Rossellini's observation that one would not perhaps otherwise suspect. The scenes of the fighting are done with great competence, and the character of the city at that time is preserved with complete integrity, but it is an episode that, one feels, De Santis or Lattuada could have done almost if not quite as well. In the fifth episode three American Army chaplains— a Roman Catholic, a Protestant and a Jew—arrive at a remote little monastery in the mountains and ask for shelter for the night. This is a most delicate little episode, humane, humorous and beautifully played, even though Bill Tubbs, as the Roman Catholic chaplain, was the only professional actor. The performances that Rossellini obtained from the monks are a mark of his genius at handling non-professional actors.

The last episode is laid in the delta of the Po, that odd, lonely, bitter, windswept place of reeds and water and sandbanks where only the wildfowlers live in their cabins built on tiny spits of sand. Here a band of Partisans and O.S.S. men, waging their savage guerilla war against the Germans, are cut off in the last stages of the war, cut off from help, and from supplies, and misled by an Allied radio order into giving away their position. They all die, shot in the lonely spaces of the marshy fenlands, hanged by the Germans or pushed overboard to drown with their hands tied behind them, or killing themselves when they realise that all hope is gone.

Paisa is a film which has all the minor faults—and all the great virtues. It is untidy, badly cut, at times almost incoherent, many of its episodes difficult to follow and making too great a demand on the audience. But what a lot remains! The balanced, economic, hopeless little tragedy of the Roman story: the warm humanity of the monastery sequences and in the last episode the mournful, empty, inhuman horizons of the delta match the isolated, hopeless but unrelentingly determined fighters, giving to the emotional content of the sequence a visual equivalent that is not only extremely beautiful in itself but which balances the feeling so perfectly that it raises it to a level of almost unbearable poignancy.[1]

Germania Anno Zero is set in the Berlin of 1947; it is the story of a German family of father, daughter, and two sons. The father is an invalid, conscious only of being a burden to his children in their struggle to survive, conscious of disaster, personal and national, that has mounted in a steady crescendo since the 1914 war. The elder son is a fugitive, never leaving the room where they live because he was one of those who fought to the last, and is afraid to surrender now. The daughter goes out to Allied clubs to dance with British and American officers who will give her cigarettes that can be bartered for food in the black market, a job that falls to the lot of the younger boy, a child of ten or eleven, but old beyond his years.

Rossellini himself says that the great artistic problem in making this

[1] When *Paisa* was shown in England in 1948 a number of the critics attacked it as anti-British, an extremely stupid and unjustifiable contention, and one which very much upset the rather over-sensitive Rossellini. It is, admittedly, the story of certain aspects of the American part of the campaign; it makes no pretence to be a history of the campaign, and in any case the British and American armies were, in general, so separated physically that contacts were comparatively limited—even in leave towns their hotels, rest camps, messes and cinemas were always separated—and it is quite certain that if it had been a British film Americans would have been equally inconspicuous. It would be completely ludicrous to label as anti-British the little vignette of the two British officers outside Florence; are we, who are so vehemently proud of our ability to laugh at ourselves, going to object when anyone else so much as smiles?

film was to get any light and shade into it. 'For us', he says, 'tragedy is a thing that comes like a storm, and then it is over. But they *live* in it. They live in tragedy like a fish in water.'

He has, though, contrived a most true and moving picture of the Berlin of 1947, its chaos, material destruction and moral breakdown, with at least two magnificent sequences. The first is that in which the younger son finds that he can make money by selling to sightseeing British and American soldiers some old gramophone records of a Hitler speech that his former schoolmaster has hidden. He sells them in the ruins of the Reichschancellerie, and no one who has seen the sequence will forget the scene in the vast, cavernous, echoing ruin, peopled only by the boy and a couple of sightseeing soldiers, when the Führer's voice shouts out from a portable gramophone 'We will always be together, in the bad days as in the good. I will never forsake the Reich. . . . '

The other episode takes up the last reel and a half of the film. The boy has put poison in his father's tea, feeling that he must give his father relief from his ever-present consciousness of being only an encumbrance to his family. For fifteen minutes or so the camera follows the boy as he wanders alone through the ruined streets, and with uncanny skill Rossellini has managed to show him living on two planes of feeling simultaneously. His body automatically joins in the game of street football which he comes across quite casually while he is preoccupied with the childish game of walking on the edge of the kerb or not stepping on the cracks between the paving stones, and then finally, when he is playing alone in an empty ruined house that was bombed before it was ever finished (a touch of symbolism?), his mind begins to brood more and more intensely on the realisation of what he has really done in poisoning his father. In the end his mind seems to arrive at the centre of an ever-narrowing circle, and he finds there the only possible solution, self-destruction, and his body hurtles down to break on the pavements far below.

A noticeable point about Rossellini's direction, more marked here than in *Roma Citta Aperta*, is the great subtlety and skill with which he hints at perversions. The slightly caressing way in which the schoolmaster slides his hand around the boy's neck, the precociously feminine attitudes of the little girl who runs about with the gang of young thieves and black-marketeers, indicate perfectly the corruption which lies hidden below the innocent-seeming surface.

66

In 1947 and 1948 Rossellini made *Amore* (*Love*). This film, originally planned to consist of three episodes, now consists of two of which only the first is one of those originally planned. This is called *La Voce Umana* (*The Human Voice*), and is based on a play by Cocteau which was originally written as a radio sketch under the title *The Telephone as an Instrument of Torture* but was subsequently turned into a one-act theatrical monologue under the title *La Voix Humaine*. It lasts for about forty minutes, during the whole of which you see Anna Magnani alone on the screen (if you except a few momentary shots of her dog), and hear no voice but hers and the occasional faint indistinguishable murmur of her ex-lover's voice over the telephone. In the writer's opinion it is one of the greatest pieces of film acting yet seen.

The film opens with Magnani bathing her face in a wash-hand basin in the bathroom of her shuttered and disordered flat; she is haggard, dishevelled, suffering (though that you only learn later) from the effects of an over-dose of a sleeping draught which she took with the intention of committing suicide. The night before the man with whom she has been living for five years had told her that to-day was the day when he was to get married, and you feel that this has torn the heart out of her existence. Now she is waiting for his telephone call to learn when he will send for the suitcases she has packed for him. When, finally, the call does come through Magnani's performance is so harrowing as to be almost unbearable. She runs the complete gamut; the feigned non-chalance that deceives no one; no, she's not been waiting for his telephone call, she's been out with Marta, no, she's slept well, she took only one sleeping pill, yes, she's quite calm now; the anguished realisation that their life together is over, posing as resigned acceptance of the inevitable; the careful facade that completely breaks down when he hangs up and she thinks the line has been disconnected, after which she calls his flat, from where he said he was speaking, to find from his servant that in fact he's somewhere else; the panic when he calls again and for a moment she can hear nothing because she wants to hear too much; the awful moment when she tries to tell him that even if he's lied to her about where he was speaking from it wouldn't matter to her, and he takes this instead as an accusation, so that she has to struggle like someone on a precipice not to let a wrangle develop; the sobs that tear her when, finding that he is going to burn her letters, she apologises for her stupid request but asks him to keep the ashes in a little cigarette box she once gave him; down to the final moment when

67

their conversation, like their life together, ends, and she is left empty and alone, her head pillowed on the telephone.

It would be easy to underestimate Rossellini's contribution; it is so unobtrusive. You might be excused for saying that all he did was to keep the camera trained on Anna Magnani while she acted. But he has, in fact, done two very important things in his direction of an episode— he has given the camera just enough mobility for the spectator not to be conscious of any monotony without ever becoming conscious that the director is playing tricks. He has given Magnani the understanding, support and sympathy which alone make such a performance possible.

It is one of the tragedies of the cinema that the appreciation of such a film is necessarily limited to those with some reasonable knowledge of Italian; Magnani's own voice is such an integral and essential part of the film that you could no more dub the film in another voice than you could make her act the part in a mask; and no subtitles could possibly convey all the shades and nuances of meaning. One of the most touching things about the dialogue is the way in which, though their love is finished, she continues to use all the *parole tenere*, the endearments used between lovers.

The other part of *Amore* is called *Il Miracolo* (*The Miracle*), and was written by one of the best Italian screen-writers, Federico Fellini. It is the story of a peasant girl who is simple rather than imbecile, and who has a trace of the madness that is sometimes respected as holy. Minding her goats on the Sorrento mountainside above the monastery where she lives she meets a bearded, good-looking tramp, and is immediately convinced that he is St. Joseph. He seduces her, and goes his way. When she finds that she is pregnant she is convinced that she has had a visitation like the Virgin Mary before her. She is mocked by the villagers, who lead her through the village in a procession singing the *Inno a Maria* and pelt her with garbage instead of flowers. She escapes from the village and lives alone in the hills till her time comes. Slowly, painfully, heavy with child, she climbs the steep mountainside to the little shrine at the top where, in a stable, she gives birth to her child. The very last shot of the film is the beautiful smile that slowly illuminates her face as she bares her breast to suckle the baby.

It is, again, a most remarkable performance by Anna Magnani, in a way more satisfactory than in *La Voce Umana* because it is less theatrical. Although it is in a very real sense a deeply religious picture it would certainly have great trouble in passing the normal censorship

68

restrictions. Physically Anna Magnani captures perfectly the appearance of the near-imbecile—the shambling run, the collection of bundles and tins that constitute her pathetic layette, her vendetta with the beggars who like her live on the monks' charity, and her garrulous self-revelations. But the real value of her performance is that through all this she contrives to let shine some essential goodness and purity of spirit of a kind denied to normal humanity, some trace of the blessed simpleton.

Once again the excellence of Rossellini's direction is in its unobtrusive adequacy on the technical side, and the skill with which he has elicited such a performance from Anna Magnani. There are, too, so many felicitous touches; the way in which, in the opening sequence, the tramp who she thinks is St. Joseph never speaks, but just smiles with carnal incomprehension at the poor imbecile telling him how beautiful he is; the way in which, pregnant but not yet conscious of the fact, the girl becomes the nursemaid of the village, gathering always about her a clutch of children in preparation for her own maternity; and her last climb up the mountain when she is accompanied by one lone goat, like her an outcast from the flock.

For this, as for all Rossellini's films, the music is by his brother Renzo Rossellini, and once again it is a perfect match. In *La Voce Umana* there are only three little musical sequences; the first introduces the film, and unerringly sets the emotional mood; the second bridges the awful moment when the man hangs up the first time, and the only slender thread that still unites the woman with her lover is broken; and the third closes the film. The rest is only the human voice, and the little noises that filter in from the flat above and the street outside. In *Il Miracolo* Renzo Rossellini's music is equally restricted to those few occasions when it will add to and not detract from the effect already made by the visual image and the spoken word.

Amore was followed by *La Macchina Amazzacattivi* (*The Machine that Kills the Wicked*). The setting of the film is Amalfi, on the Sorrento Peninsula, and the cast is partly professional and partly villagers of Amalfi and the neighbourhood. The original idea, which sprang from the fertile mind of that great Neapolitan character actor Eduardo de Filippo, is promising. A little photographer, working in a small seaside town with antiquated apparatus, discovers one day that one of his cameras has developed the power of inflicting instant death on any evil person whom he photographs, or of whom he even photographs

69

the photograph. Part of the story is concerned with his growing fascination by, and horror of, this unsought power. But mingled with this are other and not entirely homogeneous threads—the adventures in search of a room with a bath of some Americans who are seeking to exploit the commercial possibilities of the town, the internal machinations of the members of the town council, and so on.

At the time of writing (autumn 1949), there is still nothing more than a roughcut of the film in existence, and it is obvious that, apart from cutting, more scenes will have to be shot before the film can be considered complete. At present one cannot write more than that it is an unfinished film with a pleasant fantastic idea, some excellent photography, some amusing scenes, and some excellent character acting on the part of the Italian part of the cast; and that if it is ever finished it may occupy a respectable minor place in the list of Rossellini's work.

He followed this with the film which at present bears the title of *Terra di Dio* (*Land of God*), the film which stars Ingrid Bergman. With the exception of a few scenes at the concentration camp of Farfa, in the Sabina near Rome, the whole film was shot on the desolate volcanic island of Stromboli where Rossellini, Bergman, the technicians, and the cast lived for what seemed endless months in the spring and summer of 1949.

Rossellini's 1949 film, first shown publicly in 1950, was originally called *Dopo L'Uragano* (*After the Storm*), then *Terra di Dio* (*Land of God*), and finally *Stromboli* in both languages. The title variations are a pale reflection of the vicissitudes through which the film and its makers and star passed, both during the actual shooting and subsequently.

The film is the story of a woman, a European D.P., who, following her unhappy destiny through several lands, has at the opening of the film arrived at the D.P. Camp of Farfa, about fifty miles from Rome. Here she learns that her application for permission to emigrate to South America has been refused with what seems to be finality. In the reactions of despair, she marries a young Italian sailor with whom she has been having a through-the-barbed-wire flirtation, for he is a returning ex-prisoner-of-war housed in the camp adjoining hers.

He takes her to his native island of Stromboli, the first sight of which fills her with understandable despair. The black sand, the harsh rocks, the houses gradually tumbling into decay as their inhabitants

70

emigrate, never to return, the closed alien faces, and, above everything, the perpetual rumbling threat of the still-active volcano all combine to make a perpetually exacerbating framework to a marriage that in itself contains no elements of harmony or satisfaction.

The middle section of the film is taken up with the efforts of Karin (Ingrid Bergman) to achieve some sort of reasonable married life with her husband, played by Mario Vitale, a fisherman whom Rossellini found at Amalfi on the Sorrento peninsula. But she is defeated by the perpetual irritation which his crude animal vitality offers to her more refined sensibilities, and by the open hostility with which the inhabitants of the island greet her every slightest effort to depart from the strict conventional pattern of life to which they conform.

In despair she decides to leave the island and, failing to get money for that purpose from the local priest (played by Renzo Cesara, a boyhood friend of Rossellini's now living in Hollywood), she seduces the handsome young light-house keeper, a pleasure for which he rewards her with what seems an inordinately large roll of thousand-lire notes.

To escape from the island she sets out to climb over the summit of the mountain, and is trapped in one of the volcano's more violent eruptions; a night of terror and loneliness convince her that her destiny is on the island and with her husband. A new Karin therefore descends the mountain at dawn to begin a new life.

A new life—but with the same husband, on the same harsh island, with the same uncongenial and hostile neighbours? It is at this crucial point that the film lacks honesty, or at least fails to carry conviction.

It is true that one result of the long series of feuds between Rossellini and R.K.O. that dogged the making of the film was that the version shown in England and the U.S.A. was edited in America. This version has been expressly denounced by Rossellini, and it is in fact inferior in almost every respect to the Italian version edited by Rossellini himself. But even after seeing the authentic version of the film, one remains unconvinced either that Karin really suffered a transfiguring emotional experience on the mountain, or that the result (if one were prepared to accept the nature of the experience) would enable this incongruous couple to live an harmonious life together, or, finally, that this woman, who is now a spiritual as well as a physical D.P., could make any sort of home on the bleak, crude island of Stromboli. The stage has been too clearly set in the opening sequences, the

71

characters too clearly delineated. Karin has married her husband for no other reason than that he offered the only road to escape from her captivity. He is physically attracted by her, but so limited by his island up-bringing and lack of culture and education that he is quite incapable of understanding a woman of her kind. To help bridge this great gulf between them they have barely thirty words in English or Italian which they can both understand.

The film really falls between two stools. It is commercially disqualified by the fact that neither of its two principal characters is really sympathetic, while the great climax of the story lacks tension, fire, and, above all, conviction. It is artistically disqualified by the characters' lack of any psychological depth, and by a certain disquieting glibness in the invention and narration of incident.

If one excludes *Rome, Open City* (and in a certain sense it is fair to exclude it since it was made under abnormal emotional tensions), it seems that Rossellini's gifts find their most adequate expression in films made up of shorter episodes. Put *Stromboli*, *La Macchina Amazzacattivi* and *Germania, Anno Zero* in one scale, and *Paisa* and *Amore* in the other, and there is no doubt which way the balance would tilt. It is therefore both interesting and hopeful to note that the film on which Rossellini is now at work (Spring, 1950) is episodic in structure, since it is based on " The Little Flowers of St. Francis."

Chapter Seven

THE POST-WAR RENAISSANCE—PART TWO

ITALIAN post-war production falls, almost without exception, into one or other of three fairly well defined and easily recognisable categories. These may, for convenience, be called the neo-realistic, the 'super' and the commercial, and a word or two of explanation is advisable here. By neo-realistic is meant those films which have drawn their raw material from life in post-war Italy, usually treating it with great seriousness. By working almost exclusively on location and with non-professional actors, a very high degree of authenticity has been achieved; most of these films have been commercial in the sense that they were financed by ordinary commercial production companies and were intended to get back at least their costs and if possible a decent profit; the few exceptions are the two films financed by A.N.P.I. (the Italian ex-Partisan association), *Il Sole Sorge Ancora* (*The Sun Rises Again*) and *Caccia Tragica* (*Tragic Hunt*), and most of Rossellini's work. But in general the attitude of their directors was not commercial; within the limits of the story, of what the producers would stand for and what the censorship would pass, these directors sought to portray the truth as they saw it. They may not always have been completely successful, but when they failed it was generally because their vision was imperfectly realised or their artistic discipline inadequate. And while this sort of failure diminishes the artistic stature of the film as a whole it does leave intact and unspoiled many passages which not only have a degree of integrity in themselves but are not marred by being set in an insincere and incongruous frame. There is, in other words, all the difference in the world between the person who says 'It was like this ; let us show how it was', and only partially succeeds because of some weakness in his intellectual or technical equipment, and the person

73

who puts actual events into melodramatic vehicles for box-office stars.

By 'super' is meant the spectacular film whose great if not only appeal lies in costume, enormous set constructions and large crowds of extras—in short, all the panoply of the historical epic which, since the days of Guazzoni, has been as recurrent an element in the Italian cinema as the western in the American cinema.

By 'commercial' is meant those films which were intended simply to make money both by the director and the producer. It should be stated at once that nothing so stupid as a condemnation is intended by this, and in fact there have been a number of films of considerable excellence produced in Italy since the war that fall into this category; but if one is to write about them fairly it is essential to recognise that the category to which they belong is this, and not the 'neo-realistic'.

It must be admitted immediately that few, if any, of the post-war productions in the 'super' category are of any merit. *I Dieci Comandamenti* (*The Ten Commandments*), directed by Chili in 1944, can only be described as De Mille and water, the whole thing made even more dreadful by the pinchpenny air that inevitably hangs over such productions unless they have really been made almost regardless of expense. The same might with equal justice be said of Scotese's *L'Apocalisse* (*The Apocalypse*), and Zeglio's *Genoveffa di Brabante* was little better—the inclusion of two nice young Americans, Gar Moore and Harriet White, who had been perfectly at home in *Paisa*, in a heavily crêpe-haired story set in early mediaeval Germany cannot be described as an inspired piece of casting. Lux Film, one of the steadiest and most quietly competent of Italian producing companies, with such films as *Vivere in Pace* (*Living in Peace*) and *Senza Pietà* (*Without Pity*) to their credit, have had one or two attempts at the historical super with *Il Cavaliere Misterioso* (*The Mysterious Cavalier*), a story of Casanova, and a version of *Les Misèrables* called *I Miserabili*, made in two parts. But these, again, were much less successful artistically than their more modest productions on contemporary themes and almost certainly have also been less successful commercially.

In the 'super' class there remain the films of the new Italian company called Universalia. This company is headed by Salvo d'Angelo who was practically unknown in the cinema world until he made a meteoric appearance as titular head of an organisation with offices in the Castel St. Angelo, one of the historic monuments of Rome, an extremely ambitious programme embracing such names as René Clair,

Marcel l'Herbier and Gabriel Pascal, and apparently unlimited supplies of money flowing from some mysterious underground source. The first film actually made under their auspices was the comparatively modest and not very successful *Daniele Cortis*, a film which, based on Fogazzaro's famous novel, was directed by Mario Soldati, with Sarah Churchill, Gino Cervi and Vittorio Gassman in the cast. Then, getting into their stride, they launched *Fabiola*, a re-make of Cardinal Wiseman's story of ancient Rome, directed by Alessandro Blasetti, and with a star cast including Michele Morgan, Michel Simon, Massimo Girotti, and many others. Produced on an extremely lavish scale, with many millions of lire spent on the costumes and sets alone, and an almost complete disregard of time, it is certainly a very beautiful production from the photographic point of view, though its other values are more doubtful. Recorded in a mixture of French and Italian—the spoken parts dubbed into Italian for the Italian market, and vice versa—it will never have more than academic interest for students of the cinema in England and America unless dubbing becomes much more widely accepted in the near future than it has been in the past. And the film certainly cannot be classed as commercial as a film of this sort, spoken in French or Italian, is unlikely to recover more than about half of the 800,000,000 lire that is its reputed cost. *Fabiola*, which was about a year in the making, was only about half made when Universalia began their second large-scale film, yet another re-make of the already thrice made *Gli Ultimi Giorni di Pompei*, this time directed by Marcel l'Herbier and again with a mixed French and Italian cast. *Gli Ultimi Giorni* was made with an equal disregard of cost, and at an equally leisurely rate of progress. The evaluation of these two films can safely be left to time.

Much of the Italian production which falls into the 'commercial' category is, in its modest way, of considerable merit, and it is a great pity that the market for foreign films in England and even America is so specialised that most of it has little hope of ever being seen there. A fair proportion of these are historical films, usually distinguished by the easy, natural way in which directors and cast move in the past, and their happy freedom from vulgarity. Of these films at least three stand out as of considerable merit, and of these three two were directed by Soldati—*Eugenia Grandet* from Balzac's novel (the last film made by Alida Valli before she went to America, lost her Christian name, and became involved in such distressing puerilities as *Miracle of the Bells*) and *Le Miserie di Monsu Travet* from a novel by Vittorio Bersezio; the third is *Il Delitto di Giovanni Episcopo*, a re-make of d'Annunzio's story directed by Alberto Lattuada. *Eugenia Grandet*, though not very well received in Italy—some of the scenes, notably that of the death scene of Grandet père, were actually hissed at the Venice Festival in 1947—is a very solid piece of work; it suffered perhaps for reasons quite exterior to the film itself, such as the fact that the two principal characters are unsympathetic by present-day standards, while one of the basic motives of the film, miserliness, is one that is hardly understood nowadays, at least on the grand scale. But many things stand out in one's recollection of the film, particularly the sombre reality of the great rambling Grandet house. Although this was a studio-made picture the house was actually built as a whole on Scalera's biggest stage; room led into room, all of them with four walls and a ceiling; all the doors opened and shut; the windows were real windows; the passage which, in the film, leads into the great kitchen did in fact lead into the kitchen and so on, and the fact of working in the close confinement of this set may well have been responsible, at least in part, for the almost claustrophobic sense of oppression with which the spectacle of life in the Grandet household fills the spectator.

Travet is a Piedmontese dialect word for a small joist, and is used as a slang name for the lowly government employee who is one of the supports of the bureaucratic machine, the meek, downtrodden little clerk with an overbearing wife, unsympathetic colleagues and a bullying chief. It is a theme which, in the cinema, runs Cinderella a close second, but Soldati gave it life, not only by the very human and understanding way in which he built his characters up into the round instead of leaving them flat and decorated, as is so often the fate of characters in this sort of film, but also by the extraordinarily convincing way in which he places his characters right *in* the Turin of the sixties of last century. His ability to do this is indeed one of Soldati's great virtues as a director, and the city of Turin and the period of the sixties and seventies of the nineteenth century form a combination of place and time in which he is always very happily at home. Travet, his wife, and the bullying Commendatore who is Travet's chief, played respectively by Carlo Campanini, Vera Carmi and Gino Cervi, are by no means the usual theatrical players gesticulating in front of unconvincing sets; you feel that they really live, move, and have their being in the Turin of eighty years ago when it was still the seat of Government.

76

Alberto Lattuada is a director most of whose work falls in the 'neo-realistic" group, but in *Il Delitto di Giovanni Episcopo* he showed that he could also handle an historical subject very competently. A film which in period and theme has many points of resemblance with *Travet*, it has one superbly successful sequence, that in which the unhappy Episcopo, going out in search of his wife, becomes involved in the mob of pleasure-seekers celebrating the end of the old year; he is drowned in a sea of human beings as he recedes despairingly from view. Technically, though not perhaps emotionally, it bears comparison with the tremendous finale of *Les Enfants de Paradis*, and that, after all, is praise indeed.

The rest of the commercial productions need not detain us very long. Since the rather inauspicious beginning made by *Il Barbiere di Seviglia* (*The Barber of Seville*) there have been a number of films of operas: *Lucia di Lammermoor*, directed by Ballerini, with Nelly Corradi, Tito Gobbi and Italo Tajo; *L'Elisir d'Amore*, directed by Mario Costa with the same cast as *Lucia*; *Rigoletto*, directed by Carmine Gallone, with Tito Gobbi; *La Signora delle Camelie*, a filmed version of *La Traviata*, directed by Carmine Gallone, with Nelly Corradi, and, most recent, *La Redenzione di Faust*, also directed by Carmine Gallone and also with Nelly Corradi, and finished towards the end of 1948. Varying in merit, they usually have first-rate singing which is reasonably well recorded, scores that have been treated with proper respect—the rough handling which the musical critics gave to *Il Barbiere* has had a good effect—indifferent photography, and little sense of the cinema. Better than the average, in nearly every respect, is the very recently made *La Cenerentola*, shot mostly in the Royal Palace at Monza with some scenes in a great old country house near Turin; Rossini's music is beautifully played and sung, well recorded, and the camera has a sense of freedom and movement unusual in this sort of film.

There remains, in the commercial category, only one other sizable group, the films made to exploit the personality of some popular and successful stage comedian. Most of these are as bad, and as uncinematic, as you would expect, the sole exception being those built around the personality of Macario. *Come Persi La Guerra* (*How I Lost the War*) sets out to be another *Shoulder Arms*, and though of course it does not succeed in so impossible an ambition it does provide many amusing moments, and creates a lovable personality that can at least be spoken of in the same breath as Chaplin. The team that made this film, like its successor *L'Eroe della Strada* (*The Hero of the Streets*), consisted of Carlo Borghesio as director, with Steno and Monicelli to write the script. The latter are an odd couple to write the screen play of a broad, almost knockabout comedy, for Mario Monicelli was a professor of philosophy and literature until he became involved in the cinema, and he and Stefano Vanzina, a young journalist whose pen name is Steno, have together written mostly serious, rather theatrical scripts, such as *Aquila Nera* (*Black Eagle*), *La Figlia del Capitano* (*The Captain's Daughter*) from Pushkin's novel, *I Miserabili* (*Les Misèrables*) from Victor Hugo's book, and *Il Cavaliere Misterioso* (*The Mysterious Cavalier*), a film about Casanova. But for *Come Persi La Guerra* they turned out a competent broadly funny story with some delicious inventions, such as the opening scene in which Macario, as the involuntary volunteer of many wars from the Abyssinian affair on, finds himself guarding a bridge, his principal armament being a collection of all the soldier's phrase books with which he has been issued in successive campaigns, and each of which he abortively consults in turn in an effort to find a suitable phrase to address to an American; or the scene when, much later in the film, and after he had fought, if one may use such an inappropriately militaristic term for Macario's frantic search for peace at any price, with the Germans, against the Germans, with the Americans, and with the British, he meets an old comrade of the Italian army who asks him what he is doing. He starts to explain that he is carrying out reconnaissance, blunders into Italian, German, British and American military terms for his supposed activities, and ends up so muddled that not only does he forget the language in which he is supposed to be talking and the name for the thing he is supposed to be doing, but even forgets for whom he is supposed to be doing it. *L'Eroe della Strada*, made by the same team in 1948, is a step forward, and much the best Macario film to date. Here he really does begin to approach Chaplin's little man in moral stature, though many of the incidents, funny though they are, have still the air of being the invention of a team of gag men rather than of springing out of the invention and character of a single man.

In the 'neo-realistic' category the first film to support the promise of a rebirth that *Roma Citta Aperta* had made was *Sciuscia*. This was the second post-war film of De Sica, a man with a distinguished record in the theatre, but who in the cinema had never quite lived up to the promise of his quite extraordinary charm, and his obviously great intelli-

78

gence; his first post-war film was *La Porta del Cielo* (*The Door of Heaven*), a domestic tragedy of no outstanding quality. But with *Sciuscia* he found his style, as surely as Rossellini with *Citta Aperta* or Lattuada with *Il Bandito*. The opening sequences portraying the vagabond life in liberated Rome of the two shoeshine boys have a lyrical quality that is quite charming, and that adds poignancy to the squalid imbroglio in which they get involved when, comparatively innocently, they are in possession of some black-marketed American blankets when the police raid the apartment where these are being sold. But when they find themselves in prison the memories of the sunny morning rides in the Villa Borghese on their horse, which they have so proudly acquired, and of their lost freedom of the streets with its interchange of badinage with their soldier-customers and the other shoeshine boys make a tragic contrast. With rare understanding De Sica has made the real heart of the tragedy not the outward physical oppression of the boys by their harassed and overworked, rather than brutal, jailers, but the subtle corruption that starts to infect the boys themselves, the terrible ease with which, once separated, and their minds worked on by their cell mates, they become as bitter enemies as they were once close friends, everything going down into decay and death and corruption. The closing sequence of the film is perhaps as weak artistically as it certainly is technically; it is artificial and contrived in its studio effect, a contrast more striking because of the veracity of all that has preceded it. But this is a very small blemish in a film that is sensitive to a very unusual degree, and that manifests De Sica's extraordinary skill in handling children.

De Sica's only other post-war film is *Ladri di Biciclette* (*Bicycle Thieves*), a film which comes very recognisably from the same hand as *Sciuscia*. It is a film that is in the main stream of Italian post-war realism, which signifies that it is acted by non-professionals who themselves come from the environment that they represent on the screen, (a practice which, incidentally, is only possible because of the Italian practice of post-synchronisation); there is an almost total absence of studio sets and the story reflects the daily troubles, preoccupations and joys of ordinary people leading ordinary lives. It is, of course, all too possible for a film to conform perfectly to this formula and yet to have all the faults except insincerity; but not with De Sica.

His story is simplicity itself: an unemployed young married man with one child, desperately anxious for work, is offered a job which

79

demands that he shall have a bicycle. Desperately he promises to have a machine by the morrow. When his wife learns of the position she lugs the family bedding off to the municipal pawnshop to raise the necessary cash. The husband, furnished with the all-important machine, begins his work as a bill-poster, but he has hardly begun before it is stolen, and the rest of the film tells of his efforts to trace the thief and recover the treasured bicycle.

There are at least three scenes of excellent satirical comedy, one when his search for the thief leads him to a charitable institution where some well-meaning gentlefolk are dispensing religious light with thin soup, another episode when the crew of a dustcart suspend operations for the morning to help in the search, and a third when he visits a police station to report the theft and gets involved in Italian bureaucracy at its most virulent. There is an almost frightening scene when he runs the thief to earth and finds that he has brought the whole quarter about his ears. But what gives the film its principal value is the beautiful performances of the two principal players, the father (who in real life was a mechanic in the big Breda factory) and the boy who plays his son (who in real life was a Roman newsboy).

Quite a notable little contribution to the movement was made by the two films which were financed by A.N.P.I. (Associazione Nazionale Partigiani Italiani), the ex-Partisans' Association. The first of these was *Il Sole Sorge Ancora* (*The Sun Rises Again*), directed by Aldo Vergano in 1945–1946. This was a routine film of the Partisan side of the war, but distinguished by sincerity, a comparative absence of heroics, and that authenticity which so often seems to come automatically with the use of the actual scene. Their second effort was *Caccia Tragica* (*Tragic Hunt*), the remarkable first effort of a very young director, de Santis. Made in 1947 it is set in the north of Italy in that curious period immediately after peace was declared when straggling across the countryside were bands of Partisans, still armed, returning home, Republican Fascists seeking to evade capture, odd German and other deserters, and bandits posing as Partisans. The story is complicated and over-elaborate, and the acting of the principals is adequate but not much more. What gives the film its distinction is de Santis' success in capturing the atmosphere of that chaotic period when the countryside bore a strange resemblance to those periods in Italian history hundreds of years before when armed bands made life hazardous outside the big towns, and his skill in extracting an atmosphere of quite extraordinary excitement from such episodes as that of the crowd of country people closing in like a great fan on the house where the escaping Germans are hiding with their hostage, and then opening up to provide an unwilling avenue of escape as the Germans come out with their tommy guns at the ready, or the later scene of the battle between the men on the river bank and those in the boats. It is a little marred in places by some rather too fanciful directorial touches—the masks on the children's faces in the bombed house, for example—but this is only youthful exuberance, and the bare, bitter heart of the film is left unspoiled.

Outstanding among the films in this category, and well deserving of its great success, is *Vivere in Pace* (*Living in Peace*). Made in 1946–47, and directed by Luigi Zampa, the whole film was shot on a farm at Rocca Ripesena, and in the nearby village. The story is simplicity itself. While the Germans are still in occupation of the area, and the local Fascist boss is still running the village, the daughter of the farmer finds two American soldiers, one white and one coloured, the latter wounded, hiding in a wood near the farm. She brings them to the farm, where, rather unwillingly, the farmer takes them in, feeds them, and hides them. The highlight of the picture is, of course, the scene in which a German soldier visiting the farm gets riotously drunk in the kitchen while the Negro, locked up for safety in the cellar, gets riotously drunk there. The Negro breaks out and, after one agonising moment of suspense, the German hails him as a brother. Together they stage a really stupendous debauch, the farmer's whole family producing their version of boogie woogie dancing while the Negro plays hot licks on the farmer's cornet, and finally, with the wine boiling in their veins, the Negro and the German stagger down the village street arm in arm, shouting that the war is over and peace has come. Out come the villagers, first one or two timid heads, then more until the whole village joyfully pours into the street, looting from the Post which the German has abandoned the coveted flour and sugar. Morning breaks to find the whole place deserted, only the German, asleep outside his deserted and now empty Post, gradually coming back to life and consciousness and the feeling that something that was terribly right last night is terribly wrong this morning. The end of the film, when the retreating Germans shoot the farmer who has hidden the Americans—not because of this but because he has given civilian clothes to the German soldier who wants to escape—is dramatically out of key with the rest of the film, and is in particular marred by the way in which Aldo Fabrizi, who plays the

81

farmer, extracts every possible drop of melodramatic gusto from his death scene. Rossellini, one feels, would never have allowed him to get away with this. But, all said and done, the film remains in one's mind as a very real picture of very real people in a very real place, to which one looks back with the same sort of affectionate regard as to a farm where one has spent an enjoyable holiday some years ago.

A film that created a considerable stir in Italy when it was first released was *Il Bandito* (*The Bandit*), directed by Alberto Lattuada, with Anna Magnani, Carla del Poggio (in private life Signora Lattuada), Carlo Campanini, and Amedeo Nazzari in the cast. It is the story of one of the 'reduci', the returned ex-soldiers, prisoners, and refugees, who comes back to Turin from Russia to find his home destroyed, his family dispersed, and no work or place in society for himself. The first part of the story (it falls into two almost distinct halves), which deals with his bewildered efforts to re-orientate himself, is very well done, with a real feeling and sympathy for the man and his situation well and honestly portrayed. The second half, in which he becomes involved with a criminal gang, takes part in various hold-ups, and ends as the quarry of a man-hunt in the hills outside Turin, is competent melodrama but little more. Its commercial success, which was considerable, was probably due in large measure to the slight aura of scandal attaching to the episode which forms the turning-point of the film; the ex-soldier, following along the street a comely pair of legs which have attracted his attention, pursues them into a house of assignation; he explains to the madame that he wants the girl who has just come in, but when the girl appears she proves to be the sister whom he has been trying to trace. In the ensuing fight with a pimp he kills the man, and it is his subsequent flight from the police which starts him off on his short and spectacular life of crime.

Anna Magnani, after her magnificent performance in *Roma Citta Aperta* appeared in several disappointing films before again achieving anything of merit. In 1944 she was in *Quartetto Pazzo* (*Mad Quartet*), a film of little distinction directed by Salvini, and in 1945 in *Abbasso La Miseria* (*Down with Misery*); this, like *Abbasso La Richezza* (*Down with Riches*) which followed it in early 1947, was a fairly robust comedy using for its raw material the antics of the black marketeers and new rich who were so prominent in Italian life at that time. Both films were directed by Righelli, and are by no means without merit; they have a considerable measure of honesty, score some shrewd hits, and have a

82

lively rhythm. But they are not so much a waste of Magnani's talent as destroyed by their failure to use it.

In 1947 came the first film worthy of her talents since *Citta Aperta*. This was *L'Onorevole Angelina* (*Angelina M.P.*), the film with which Zampa followed *Vivere in Pace*. It is set in one of those shoddy little working-class housing estates which the Fascists built with a great fanfare of trumpets shortly before the War, and which have rapidly degenerated into the slums that were their obvious destiny.

Among the people living here is a lowly, underpaid, harassed police official, beautifully played by Nando Bruno, his wife, played by Anna Magnani, and their five children. The wife's constant preoccupation is to manage somehow or other to fill the six clamouring stomachs—her own is too well disciplined to clamour—with prices always rising and the policeman's wage stationary. The breaking-point comes when the proprietor of the general shop, the only one in the area, refuses to issue the ration of *pasta* the macaroni that is the essential basis, and often the superstructure as well, of the poor Italian's food. Angelina rebels, and leads a mob of women to storm the warehouse behind the shop where the *pasta* is stored. In this act she suddenly finds herself, and becomes the acknowledged leader and champion of all the women of the neighbourhood.

When the floods come to the low-lying area where the estate was built, so that they all have to escape in boats, it is Angelina who leads them, her devoted followers in any enterprise, to occupy a nearly-finished but unoccupied block of flats near by. Angelina, taken to prison, is bailed out by the owner of the block who has good reason to fear too close an investigation of his affairs by the authorities. He persuades Angelina to withdraw her troops, and then proceeds subtly to compromise her, so that her once-devoted band of followers now regard her with suspicion and distrust, eventually to be won back to their allegiance. Anna Magnani plays the part as no one else in any country could do; she constructs a character that is intensely human, a memorable portrait of a woman of the people, crude, shrill, with a flow of invective in the choicest Romanesque and a heart of gold where her family is concerned. Zampa, whose work in *Vivere in Pace*, *L'Onorevole Angelina* and *Anni Difficili* (*Difficult Years*) puts him right in the front rank, showed in this film that he is the only Italian director other than Rossellini who can get (or perhaps permit) a first-class performance

83

from Anna Magnani and who can also construct a frame which can stand up to such a portrait.

A number of films have, with varying merit, dealt with the seamier side of Italy's post-war troubles, amongst them *Tombolo, Paradiso Nero (Tombolo, Black Paradise), Senza Pietà (Without Pity)*, and *Gioventù Perduta (Lost Youth)*. *Tombolo*, directed by Ferroni, and starring Aldo Fabrizi, was an extremely lurid and not very well-made film about the notorious Tombolo wood near Leghorn, where deserters, criminals and prostitutes lived like twentieth-century outlaws, a bunch of sordid, diseased and worthless Robin Hoods. *Senza Pietà*, directed by Alberto Lattuada, and with a cast including Carla del Poggio, John Kitzmiller (the Negro of *Vivere in Pace*), Folco Lulli and Pierre Claude, deals with exactly the same theme but very much better. The film is greatly helped by the desperate sincerity of Carla del Poggio and John Kitzmiller's acting, distinguished as it is by some very convincing and veracious backgrounds, and marred only by a rather conventional presentation of the gang leader, played by Pierre Claudè. *Gioventù Perduta* deals with the themes of the thrill-seeking, money-hungry youth of the generation that was at school during the war years. It ran into trouble with the censorship authorities, who took a not unreasonable exception to the very detailed way in which the planning and execution of various armed hold-ups were shown. Directed by Pietro Germi the players include Jacques Sernas as the youthful criminal, Massimo Girotti as the detective who is tracking him down, and Carla del Poggio as the undergraduate's sister and sweetheart of the detective.

Two more films that come into the 'neo-realistic' category call for some detailed consideration. The first is *La Terra Trema (The Earth Trembles)*, the most controversial and most discussed film of the 1948 Venice Festival. It was directed by Luchino Visconti, his only film since *Ossessione* in 1942, and was announced as the first part of a trilogy following the plan of Giovanni Verga's trilogy on which it is based. This part, which deals with the life of Sicilian fishermen, was to be followed by two others dealing respectively with the lives of Sicilian peasants and miners. The film is extremely long, rather obscure in action, and practically incomprehensible in dialogue; so broad is the dialect that even educated Sicilians are frequently at a loss.

The film was ostensibly made by Universalia and produced by Salvo d'Angelo, but there is overwhelming internal evidence that there was no producer at all. It is a perfect example of the work of a gifted serious

84

director running completely wild. Visconti possibly made the film with his own money, and used Universalia simply as a convenient cloak. It is certainly a little odd that a company with such close connections as Universalia has with the richer and more authoritative orders of the Roman Catholic Church, should have sponsored a film whose sympathy for the downtrodden and exploited poor should be as outspoken as this. The photography is never less than good and is frequently brilliant; the extreme harshness of the Sicilian light makes it often difficult to avoid a very flat effect, so that a mountainside will seem almost like a theatrical back cloth, but these difficulties have been magnificently overcome by G. R. Aldo. The acting, if such a word is appropriate, of the Sicilian fishermen and villagers—there are no actors in the cast— is often good, though not always free from self-consciousness. All that can be said at present is that the film contains a mine of documentary material which, if Visconti can bring himself to cut ruthlessly enough, may one day make a film not unworthy to stand beside *Nanook* and *Finis Terrae*.

With *Anni Difficili* (*Difficult Years*) Zampa has brought off a triumphant success; it is a completely worthy companion to *Vivere in Pace* and *L'Onorevole Angelina*, and an extremely courageous film. Based on Vitaliano Brancati's well-known novel *Il Vecchio con gli Stivali* (*The Old Man with the Boots*), it is the story of a petit bourgeois family during the years of Fascism and war. The father of the family, superbly played by Umberto Spadaro, is a small local-government official in Palermo, who unwillingly becomes a nominal Fascist because otherwise he will lose his job. His wife and daughter take to the movement much more enthusiastically; his son, seeking only a chance to settle down, get a job and marry, is involved in one 'glorious Fascist adventure' after another, 'volunteer' for Abyssinia, 'volunteer' for Spain, then off to Albania, Greece and Russia, returning home at long last only to be brutally shot down in wanton cold-bloodedness by the retreating Germans.

Zampa has held a very fine balance between the comic invention that fills all his work with such humanity, the petty frustrations and stupidities of provincial Fascism, and the framework of universal tragedy in which the whole is set. He has, very wisely, made the most of the many ludicrous aspects of Fascism, realising that to bring laughter to bear on such subject is like opening the windows of a diseased and morbid household to the disinfecting sun; and with remarkable fairness he has

85

shown the division of the town into the active, sincere and fanatic Fascists, those who joined only for peace and quiet out of sheer self-preservation, and the dissident minority who confined themselves to grumbling behind closed doors.

The very end of the film is typical of its half-bitter, half-ironic tone. The father, who became a Fascist only when the alternative was to lose his job, was fitted out by his ambitious wife with the special insignia reserved for the *Vecchia Guardia*, the Old Guard who made the famous 'March' on Rome. When A.M.G. takes over the town, the American Town Major, a beautiful portrait of a political imbecile aided by the ex-Fascist Mayor who is his trusted and invaluable right-hand man, seizes the insignia as evidence of the old man's guilt, and sternly pronounces him unworthy to share in a democratic administration. Slowly, sadly, brokenly, the old man goes out into the street outside; it is filled with shouting, celebrating, raucous American soldiery; one G.I. has come across the old man's fatal Vecchia Guardia uniform, and is busy selling it to another G.I. for five bucks. The buyer festoons himself in the uniform while his friend takes the inevitable snapshot. Nobody notices the little old man, with his head in his hands, sitting on the kerb at their feet.

Before we leave the new realist school we must discuss the work of the individualistic director Francesco de Robertis. For each of the seven films he has made so far he has acted as his own producer, has written the story and dialogue from his own original idea, and has even written the whole of the music for one film and part of the music for others. Nor has he ever used a professional actor or actress in any of his films with the exception of Gandusio, who has a small part in *Marinai Senza Stelle* (*Sailors without Stars*); but then Gandusio plays the part of an actor, so in a sense he, like the rest, was only impersonating himself.

De Robertis was a career naval officer when, in 1938, the Italian Ministry of Marine selected him as technical adviser of a documentary film they were planning on methods of escape from submarines in difficulty. De Robertis' own ideas were less modest and he was determined to make a full-length feature, and not a mere documentary. Scalera, who had provided the technical crew, refused their consent on the grounds of his inexperience; the Ministry of Marine did likewise. Nothing daunted, de Robertis went ahead with permission from nobody; by the time the authorities realised what was happening de Robertis had piled up such an impressive footage of film that, resignedly, they let him finish what he had begun. The result was *Uomini sul Fondo* (*Men in the Deep*), a well-made, very exciting, and technically polished story about the crew of a submarine which goes down for an endurance test and then is damaged when surfacing. *Uomini sul Fondo* was made in 1939; his next two films, naturally enough, were also on naval topics, *La Nave Bianca* (*The White Ship*) and *Alfa Tau*. For *Uomini sul Fondo* the Scalera technicians had insisted on reconstructing the divided half of a submarine interior; they said it was technically impossible to make a film inside a real submarine. By the time he came to make *Alpha Tau* de Robertis knew better, and like a good Italian realist he shot all the submarine interior scenes for that film inside a real submarine.

Alfa Tau was made in 1942. In 1943 de Robertis made *Uomini e Cieli* (*Men and Skies*), a film, below his usual standard, about four Italian Air Force pilots, and *Marinai Senza Stelle* (*Sailors Without Stars*), a most charming little film about the boys of a naval school with at least two unforgettable scenes; the first is that in which the boys climb out of their dormitory at night to fight a mock battle between the two factions into which the school is divided for the possession of their ship; this scene, with the boys swarming all over the ship in the moonlight, is one of those scenes, so rare in the cinema and so satisfactory, when the visual beauty of the scene exactly matches the emotional content, and by its matching heightens both enormously. The other scene is very different; it is a courtroom scene, for the relatives of two of the orphan boys at the school have got themselves involved in some very heated litigation over a boat they were supposed to be building together. This little scene is a gem of the purest natural comedy, with not a line nor a grimace nor a gesture overplayed; not one of the characters had ever seen a camera before in his life; not one performance is less than perfect, and it establishes de Robertis as yet another Italian director capable of getting magnificent performances from ordinary people.

His last films to date are *La Vita Semplice* (*The Simple Life*) and *Fantasmi del Mare* (*Ghosts of the Sea*). The latter, a heavily naval theme, is competently handled but not especially interesting to the layman. *La Vita Semplice*, on the other hand, is a delight. It is really a fable, with a lovely rhythmic proportion in its construction. The film opens with a gondola peacefully making its time-unaltered way along the Grand Canal in Venice; it is nearly upset by the wash from the speeding launch of an industrialist who builds motorboats, and who symbolises all that is hasty, angry, preoccupied in our way of life. For an extension to his factory he needs the land where the boat builder whom he has nearly upset pursues leisurely, happily and philosophically his traditional boat building. But the boat builder won't sell. Why should he? He has enough to live on. He doesn't want to move—he's lived there all his life, and intends to die there. He doesn't want to retire—he wants to go on building gondolas, peacefully, happily, without undue haste.

The conflict, counterpointed by a love affair between the boat builder's son and the industrialist's daughter, is explored in the film with a rich delight in the variety and ultimate absurdity of humanity, and the final sequence brings the whole fable to a nicely rounded close. The young couple are wed, and have departed in the bridal gondola. Down the canal after them float the now reconciled fathers, the boat builder ceremoniously decked out in his best, the industrialist relaxing in unaccustomed democratic ease. Suddenly their gondola is violently rocked by the wash of a speeding launch, and the last we see of the industrialist he is vigorously cursing this blatant and insensitive disturber of the Venetian peace.

Chapter Eight

A NOTE ON DOCUMENTARY

THE world of Italian documentary is, to one used to British factual films, a very strange world indeed. Put simply, the sociological documentary, which makes up in England the greater part of this branch of production along with films which are purely instructional, simply does not exist.

There are various reasons for this difference. One is that the Government prefers to spend what little money it can devote to things of the spirit to subsidising opera at the Caracalla Baths or the Opera House, or to encouraging motor racing, or to helping the International Horse Show or the Venice Festival, rather than to making films at £2,000 a reel to show little Giovanni how to brush his teeth, or Maria his mother the best way to make plum jam. Another reason is more fundamental; in Britain the civic spirit is very highly developed, whereas in Italy there is an intense local patriotism, which is something quite different. Yet a further reason is that owing to the comparative lack of sponsors for documentary films the only ones that get made are those which somebody really wants to make for his own personal satisfaction, and which stand at least some chance of being booked by the ordinary commercial cinema and thus qualifying for the 3 per cent rebate on the box-office takings which is what, financially speaking, really saves the day.

Discounting the one and only Italian newsreel, Incom, the overwhelming majority of Italian documentaries come into the 'art film' class; they consist, that is, of photographs of pictures, statues, buildings, and less often of landscapes. And in this field the names of Luciano Emmer and Enrico Gras stand out as pre-eminently as that of Rossellini among the realists.

Luciano Emmer, with his wife and a friend Enrico Gras as collaborators, began producing experimental documentaries in the last few years before the outbreak of the Second World War. His ideas on documentary were so greatly at variance with the official Fascist point of view—his commissioned film on *Land of Mussolini's Birth* was so surrealistic that the only part the officials understood was the woman in black, carrying a scythe, who wandered about the landscape—that he found absence the better part of discretion, and quietly removed himself to Switzerland. After some unpleasant experiences which included a period in a German concentration camp, he came back to Italy, and made a fresh start. This time everything went well.

The first film that the team completed was called *Il Dramma di Cristo* and consisted entirely of photographs of the famous Giotto frescoes at Padova. But Emmer and Gras in photographing these murals did what has never been done before, and had probably never even been attempted. They did not simply photograph the murals in a series of alternating long shots, medium shots, and close ups; they took the whole thing to pieces and put it together again, achieving cinematically the effect at which Giotto himself was aiming statically. Without entering into art criticism, it seems permissible to claim that Giotto was trying to do two things simultaneously—to tell the story of Christ, more particularly his flight to Egypt as a child, his raising of Lazarus from the dead, and his betrayal and crucifixion, and at the same time to create objects of plastic beauty. Emmer and Gras, taking the objects of plastic beauty as they found them, used them to re-tell the story so that the result on a twentieth-century mind is very much that which the original must have had on the fourteenth-century minds who first saw them.

The director of a normal film, engaged in realising such a scene as, for example, the massacre of the Innocents, would have a shooting script that would read something like this, omitting for simplicity much of the detail :—

247. Long Shot. Soldiers marching.
248, 249, 250. Same as above.
251. Medium shot of soldier drawing sword.
252. Medium shot of mother trying to protect child.
253. Close up of soldier's face.
254. Close up of sword descending.
255. Medium shot of heap of children's bodies: another corpse
     is flung on to the heap.

90

Emmer and Gras have shot this scene exactly as a first-class director would have done, using however the figures and objects painted by Giotto instead of live actors and real things. They create a sense of movement and rhythm out of static objects by having the camera practically always moving, and by shooting from exactly the angle which will give them the effect they are seeking. A particularly striking example of this is in the final scene when, by photographing an angel from a series of gradually changing angles, never holding one angle for more than a few frames, they achieve a most beautifully stylised effect of flight.

Made in the same way, and equally successful, was their film of the Hieronymus Bosch tryptych at Madrid of the banishment of Adam and Eve. Shortly after this they made yet another considerable step forward in their *Sulla Via di Damasco*; for this, which tells the story of the life of St Paul, they ranged far and wide in their choice of material— maps, paintings, frescoes, statues were all brought into use, and the result is one of the most richly satisfying examples of their work in this vein.

After this they made something of a break, and their next documentary was a film of the allied war cemeteries in Italy called *Bianchi Pascoli* (*White Pastures*); while not perhaps on quite as high a level as their preceding work, it would certainly be accepted as good documentary anywhere with a genuinely fresh approach, visually as well as spiritually, to a subject that is not easily susceptible of fresh treatment. They followed this up with two charming studies of Venice, the first called *I Romantici di Venezia* (*The Romantics of Venice*), and the second *Isole della Laguna* (*Islands of the Lagoon*); the first is a series of photographic studies of those parts of Venice associated with such well-known romantic figures as Byron, de Musset and George Sand. It contains one outstanding sequence the whole of which consists of the reflections in the waters of the canals of the buildings which the gondola is passing. *Isole della Laguna* is an equally charming survey of the islands in the Venetian lagoon.

The general trend of Italian documentary production, however, has great uniformity; long lists of films celebrating in static splendour the architecture and art of Italy.

Two honourable exceptions to this sad uniformity must be named. One is Panaria Film, a Sicilian producing house which is the private preserve of a family of rich Italian dilettanti, Prince Alliata and his

91

brother in particular. They have made nothing but documentaries, and only a few of those. The best, and they are outstandingly good, are *Tonnara* (*Tunny Fishing-ground*), a study of the Sicilian tunny fishermen at work: *Isole di Cenere* (*Islands of Ashes*), a beautifully photographed record of the extinct volcanic islands in the area of Sicily: and *Cacciatori Sottomarini* (*Underwater Hunters*), an exciting and very well photographed account of the Italian sport of shooting fish under water with a spring-gun that fires a harpoon, the hunter wearing a mask to aid his sight but having no artificial means of breathing[1]. The second honourable exception is Cortometraggi, of Milan. Out of their comparatively small production two documentaries stand out, *Bambini in Città* (*Children in the City*) and *Cortili* (*Courtyards*), both directed by Dino Risi. The first is a study of the life of poor children in a big city, any big city, and is distinguished by a sympathy that interprets the whole subject with comprehension and pity. *Cortili* is a series of very plainly photographed studies of the courtyards round which nearly all the life of the poorer sections of Italian towns revolves; it is distinguished by the same impersonal, almost Olympian, sympathy as the earlier film, and has a most interesting sound track consisting only of natural sound recorded on the spot—the only music is that picked up from a radio heard through an open window, a woman singing, an accordion player, and so on.

Finally, there is a most intellectually exciting documentary called *Una Lezione in Geometria*, and the full list of credit titles should for once be given. It was produced by Carlo Ponti, directed by Virgilio Sabel with Bianca Lattuada as executive producer; the music was by Goffredo Petrassi and the photography by Mario Bava. But the whole thing is really the conception of Leonardo Sinisgalli, a contemporary Italian poet and professor of mathematics; he made the film, and probably c⁻¹⁷ a man who was both a poet and a mathematician could have created it.

Beginning with a spoken quotation from Lautrémont it shows a machine tracing a series of ellipses, explains with beautiful clarity the geometric basis of the ellipse, and the algebraic formula for calculating the position of any point on it; from this point it sets off to explore, with the most logical fantasy, the infinite variety of complex shapes that occur in science, and the even more complex shapes that we find in

[1] Sections of all these three documentaries have been cut into Dieterle's *Vulcano* with Anna Magnani and Rossano Brazzi.

Nature—the fantastic geometry of the crystal, the extraordinary perfection of the egg, the relation between the curves traced by the cathode ray oscillograph and the movements of the heavenly bodies, and ends up, after a diversion by way of the human skeleton, by establishing the correspondence between the work of such modern artists as Archipenko, Brancusi, Picasso and Moore, and some of the more complex figures we had been studying a few minutes ago. It is photographed with great skill and beauty, and has an admirably written commentary.

Chapter Nine

SOME NOTES ON ITALIAN DIRECTORS
AND ITALIAN PRODUCTION METHODS

ROBERTO ROSSELLINI was born in 1906 in Rome, a city where, with the exception of his 1947 trip to Germany to make *Germania Anno Zero*, he has lived all his life. His father was a building contractor who was reasonably well off and Rossellini, like many other Italian young men, felt under no particular compulsion to work. But in 1935 the family affairs declined, and Roberto was faced with the necessity of doing something to support himself. He drifted into the cinema world almost by chance, and more because he had friends and acquaintances in that milieu than for any more definite reason; certainly he was conscious of nothing like a vocation. He began as a dubbing technician, again largely by chance, and continued for some time in various not very exalted jobs on the technical side of dubbing; his apprenticeship to this side of film making lasted four years, and it was not until 1939 that he became a director and made his first film, a documentary about fish.

He spent some time making documentaries of one sort or another before getting his first chance to make a full-length film; his first essay in normal direction was on de Robertis' *Nave Bianca*, but he and de Robertis disagreed very violently, and the latter finished the film by himself and removed Rosellini's name from the list of credits. His next film was *Un Pilota Ritorna* (*A Pilot Returns*), one of the usual propaganda films of those days.

Shortly after this he was suspended from the Consorzio dei Registi, the Fascist trades union for directors, membership of which was essential if a director wanted to get work. He left Rome for six weeks, coming back on the fateful 8th of September, 1943, the day of the Armistice.

94

Two aspects of his work as a director seem rather odd in conjunction; the first is his ability, not uncommon in good Italian directors, to coax extremely natural performances from people untrained as actors; the second is his ability to get from professional actors and actresses better performances than anyone else can get. Anna Magnani has never equalled the work she gave for him in *Roma Citta Aperta* and *Amore*, nor Aldo Fabrizi his performance in *Roma Citta Aperta*, nor Maria Michi hers in *Roma Citta Aperta* and *Paisa*; when they work for other directors they seem, in comparison, almost to lose a dimension of their characters.

The overwhelming preoccupation of Rossellini's life is to maintain his independence. As a result of this he refuses to sign contracts to direct for any normal company, and spends more time in search of backers who will allow him to make the film he wants to make in the way he wants to make it than he does in actually making the film. But since the ultimate result is such films as *Germania Anno Zero*, *Amore*, and *La Macchina Amazzacattivi*, and since it is quite certain that such films could not get made any other way, we must applaud his single-minded determination.

As a director he is very quiet, frequently seeming lost in thought from which he emerges with the necessary inspiration, the obvious idea that no one else has had, and he has, as might be deduced from his films, the art of winning his actors' confidence to an extraordinary degree. Shooting a film is only the beginning for him; he lives with the film for months afterwards, doing most of the cutting himself, and superintending the later technical stages in considerable detail. He is one of the few directors who have realised that what the public sees is not what goes in the lens of the camera but what comes out of the lens of the projector, and that a director who is serious about his work has as much to do after the rushes have been developed and printed as before.

LUIGI ZAMPA is that rare bird, a director who is equally popular with the public because of the humanity and humour of his films, and with his producers because they hardly ever fail to make a profit.

After a number of routine films he began to show his quality in *Un Americano in Vacanza* (*An American on Holiday*), a film of American soldiers on leave in Italy about the time the campaign ended; light without being frivolous, it showed the promise which he quickly made good in *Vivere in Pace*. His work is showing an increasing depth, *L'Onorevole Angelina* and *Anni Difficili* being both films in which a frequently light surface does not obscure an essentially serious attitude.

MARIO SOLDATI was born in Turin in November 1906. He studied with the Jesuits, and later took an Arts degree at Turin University. In 1929 he went to Columbia University as a teacher and student combined— to teach the history of art and to learn the language. He acquired a grasp of the English language which makes it, in his hands, a very vigorous if slightly uncertain weapon which he wields with enormous gusto and occasionally devastating effect.

He spent some time assisting Camerini, and then began writing scripts, an art in which he acquired some skill, for he has a decidedly literary turn. It was not until 1937 that he directed his first film, *La Principessa Tarakanova*; this was six years or so after he had entered the film world, but in the interval he had written three books as well as a number of scripts, in addition to his directing duties, so he had not been idle. His first three films had only a middling, or less than middling, success, but in his fourth he really found himself; he also found Alida Valli. The film was *Piccolo Mondo Antico (Little Old-fashioned World)*, and was based on the novel by Fogazzaro, a writer with whom he has always had a great affinity. The period is the Risorgimento, in which he has always liked to work, and the action is set in Turin and the Italian lakes, districts in which he is very much at home. The film deserved its success for it was very sensitively directed, well acted, and contained many moments of extreme visual beauty.

Soldati's literary bias is evident in his choice of subjects. After *Piccolo Mondo Antico*, which was made in 1940, he made *Malombra*, from another Fogazzaro novel in 1942; in 1944–45 he made *Le Miserie di Monsu Travet (The Miseries of M. Travet)*, based on Vittorio Bersezio's novel, written in 1862; in 1945–46 *Eugenia Grandet*, based on Balzac's novel, and in 1946–47 *Daniele Cortis*, again from a book by Fogazzaro.

In 1948 he made a bid to break away from what he felt was becoming a rut by directing for Lux a film called *Fuga in Francia (Flight into France)*; Soldati himself had written a book with this title but the coincidence was fortuitous; the screen play was written by himself in collaboration with Carlo Musso and Ennio Flaiano, and is the story of a collaborationist and his attempt to escape from justice. The film is only moderately successful, though this is due less to weaknesses in

96

Soldati's work than to the fact that Folco Lulli, who plays the principal part, is the sort of actor who is adequate only in supporting parts.

In addition to directing and writing Soldati is an actor, and frequently takes minor parts in his own and other people's films; his professor in Castellani's *Mio Figlio Professore* (*My Son, the Professor*) was a small but outstanding performance.

MARIO CAMERINI is one of the senior of the Italian directors now regularly making films. His first film of any importance, *Rotaie* (*Rails*), was made in 1929, and his next *Figaro e La Sua Gran' Giornata* (*Figaro's Great Day*), made in 1931, was a great success. His work before and during the war was always competent, and frequently revealed with engaging humanity and genuine understanding the humours of the petit bourgeois life that had a particular appeal for him. His best films of this period were *Gli Uomini Che Mascalzoni* (*What Rascals Men Are*), *Darò un Milione* (*I'll Give a Million*), *Ma Non E una Cosa Seria* (*But It's Nothing Serious*), *Il Signor Max, Batticuore* (*Heart-throb*), and *Una Romantica Avventura* (*A Romantic Adventure*).

After the war his work took a turn for the more serious, as his first post-war film, *Due Lettere Anonime* (*Two Anonymous Letters*), showed. Set in German-occupied Rome, it is a drama which, like so much of Camerini's work, ends with a note of pardon and sober hope that is never mere sentimentality. He followed this with *La Figlia del Capitano* (*The Captain's Daughter*), an historical Russian romance taken from Pushkin's novel. This is sound and workmanlike, but not much more, and his latest film, *Molti Sogni per Le Strade* (*The Streets Have Many Dreams*) was an attempt, not entirely successful, to establish himself in the neo-realist school. His handling of Massimo Girotti in this film was rather wooden, while Anna Magnani's performance was, one felt, perhaps unjustly, exactly what she would have done had there been no director there at all. As a director he is, like Soldati, very dependent on having a subject which strikes some spark of lively sympathy in his heart, but he is not as firm as he should be in choosing only such subjects for his work.

ALBERTO LATTUADA was born in Milan in 1914, studied as an architect, and designed a cinema pavilion for the Triennale Festival in Milan. His first work in the cinema was as assistant director and script writer to Soldati on *Piccolo Mondo Antico*. His first film, *Giacomo*

L'Idealista (*Giacomo the Idealist*), was widely praised for its original and felicitous direction. He followed this up in 1943 with *La Freccia nel Fianco* (*The Arrow in the Side*), but the first film with which he really made his mark was *Il Bandito* (*The Bandit*), which he directed in 1946. In this he definitely established his claim to be one of the three principal directors of the new realist school; if Rossellini is the poet of the school and Zampa the humanist, then Lattuada is the man of action and incident. His work is always tightly packed, active and well documented. His style has a hard, brilliant surface that is not unpleasing, and when he turns to historical subjects, as he did with *Il Delitto di Giovanni Episcopo* (*The Crime of Giovanni Episcopo*) from d'Annunzio's novel, which he made in 1947, it serves him equally well. He followed this with a return to a modern theme, *Senza Pieta* (*Without Pity*), a story of the Negro and white army deserters, prostitutes, blackmarketeers and gangsters who infested Leghorn during the last few months of the war and the early post-war period, a film which is restrained from melodrama only by Lattuada's very firm grasp of reality and his sense of character.

ALESSANDRO BLASETTI shares with Camerini, whose contemporary he is, the honour of being the doyen of the directors who are still working.

An ebullient and vital director, he is at his best in historical films, as one of his earliest successes, *1860*, showed; although made in 1933, this story of Garibaldi and his Thousand is still in many ways a model of what such a film should be. As though to display his virtuosity, he made among a number of heavy historical pictures such as *Corona di Ferro* (*Crown of Iron*), the little sentimental comedy, *Quattro Passi Fra Le Nuvole* (*A Stroll in the Clouds*), a film made with great charm, simplicity, and freshness. After the war he made *Un Giorno nella Vita* (*A Day of Life*), a harsh and dramatic story of the massacre by the Germans of a convent of Enclosed nuns. Soon after that was finished he started on the preliminary work for the gigantic *Fabiola*, the active direction of which occupied him for practically the whole of 1948. He has the reputation of being one of the most extravagant of Italian directors, but at least he usually produces value for the money, and he handles with great skill those crowd scenes which usually account for a good part of his swollen (by Italian standards) budget, while his long experience and deep knowledge of the technique of film making enable him to get the best possible technical results out of the people who work with him.

British and American technicians are usually astonished when they see the equipment with which most Italian directors have to work—the fluctuating and inadequate supplies of current, the shortage of good arcs and the general inadequacy of their lighting equipment, their primitive microphone booms and patched-up sound channels, the old cameras and the studio roofs devoid of gantries.

One must in many ways applaud the Italians for their common sense in making-do with what they have. Quantities of expensive equipment can only be justified economically when there is a constant high level of production, which there is not in Italy. Otherwise it would only be a means of adding to their films an extra technical gloss which would not bring in an extra lire in any of their markets; for technical excellence is not what draws people to see the kind of films they make best. In their domestic market, and the other European markets open to them, a limit to their revenue is set by the greater counter-attraction of American, and to a lesser extent British stars. Glossier pictures will not help them to develop stars rivalling Ingrid Bergman, Spencer Tracy and James Mason in their box office appeal. Nor will they help them, in America, Britain, and the English-speaking countries generally, to break out of the closed circle of specialist cinemas; at least not until the conservative audience objections to dubbing are overcome, for the sub-titled original version of a foreign language film seems unlikely ever to appeal to a mass audience.

Italian films have been so widely, and rightly, praised for their realism that it is interesting to attempt to analyse its causes. Its basic cause is undoubtedly the greater realism of the Mediterranean outlook on life, compared with the rather cloudier outlook in the Anglo-Saxon countries. The prostitute in *Paisa is* a prostitute; she wheedles a drunken soldier to her room and proceeds to take off her clothes; when the husband in *Ossessione* gets drunk he *does* get drunk, and lurches off to the side of the road to vomit; when Anna Magnani in *Il Miracolo* finds that she is pregnant she has pains in her belly, not a beatific smile on her face as she gets out knitting materials to start on the customary 'little things'. This is a really fundamental difference in the outlook of the Mediterranean nation as compared with the British and American outlook; it is the outlook of a country that considers

99

wine and good food as more important than dog tracks, and the family as the basis of life; for it is a country that is still basically peasant, or little and but recently removed from the peasant, and the peasant in every country has this sound grasp on the basis of existence.

A secondary, but important cause, is that the comparative smallness of film budgets in Italy compels directors to do most of their shooting in front of the real thing, instead of painfully and expensively reconstructing it in the studio. This is much more practicable in Italy than it would be in England or even in America, because the climate is in general so stable that little shooting time is lost on location. The very great variety of scenery and architecture in a comparatively small area is another factor for economy; you can, if you like and if your script demands, shoot a ski-ing sequence in the morning and a sea bathing one in the same afternoon; mediaeval castles, towns untouched since the Middle Ages, Palladian villas, Venetian palaces are all there for the asking, and the fact that every Italian is a natural actor makes the selection of character-extras on the spot easy for the casting director.

The Italian director's habit of working with non-professionals is partly because, with only a few actors and actresses to choose from, ringing the changes soon induces both monotony and lack of conviction, and partly because people in their own habitual surroundings can usually be coaxed by a sympathetic director to give very natural performances. This is aided by the fact that it is the almost invariable practice for Italian films to be shot mute, sometimes with a guide track, sometimes without even that, and for the entire sound-track to be post-synchronised in the studio; in this way the non-professional, who can usually manage his body, rarely his voice, and practically never the two together, is spared the embarrassment of a microphone, and his part is dubbed for him in the studio by one of Italy's innumerable skilful dubbers.

Finally, and it is a point of some considerable importance, the Italian director has in general more authority than his English counterpart, and suffers infinitely less from producer-interference than his American colleagues. He usually plays a very large part in the casting of the film, and more often than not his name appears as one of the authors of the screen play. The fact that Italian producing houses are very small, almost family affairs compared with the British and American companies, makes it much easier for the director to get his personal point of view accepted.

100

Appendix I.

A LIST OF ITALIAN FILMS DIRECTED FROM 1930-1948
BY THE LEADING DIRECTORS

*ALESSANDRO BLASETTI
  Sole, 1928.
  Resurrectio, 1930.
  Nerene, 1930.
  Terra madre, 1930.
  Palio, 1932.
  1860, 1933.
  La tavola dei poveri, 1932.
  Il caso Haller, 1933.
  L'impiegata di papà, 1933.
  Vecchia guardia, 1934.
  Aldebaran, 1935.
  La contessa di Parma, 1937.
  Ettore Fieramosca, 1938.
  Retroscena, 1939.
  Un' avventura di Salvator Rosa, 1940.
  La corona di ferro, 1941.
  La cena delle beffe, 1941, (?).
  Quattro passi fra le nuvole, 1942.
  Nessuno torna indietro, 1943.
  Un giorno nella vita, 1946.
  Fabiola, 1948.

*MARIO CAMERINI
  Rotaie, 1929.
  Kiff Tebbi, 1933.
  Figaro e la sua gran giornata, 1931.
  La figlia del Capitano, 1948.
  Molti sogni per la stradà, 1948.
  L'ultima avventura, 1932.
  Gli uomini, che mascalzoni, 1932.
  T'amerò sempre, 1933.
  Cento di questi giorni, 1933.
  Giallo, 1933.
  Come le foglie, 1934.
  Il cappello a tre punte, 1934.
  Darò un milione, 1935.
  Ma non e una cosa seria, 1936.
  Il grande appellè, 1936.

Il signor Max, 1937.
  Batticuore, 1939.
  Grandi magazzini, 1939.
  Il documento, 1939.
  100,000 *dollari*, 1940.
  Una romantica avventura, 1940.
  I promessi sposi, 1941.
  Una storia d'amore, 1942.
  T'amerò sempre (nuova edizione), 1943.
  Due lettere anonime, 1944.
  L'angelo e il diavolo, 1944.

RENATO CASTELLANI
  Un colpo di pistola, 1942.
  Zazà, 1943.
  La donna della Montagna, 1943.
  Mio figlio professore, 1946.
  Sotto il sole di Roma, 1948.

*MARIO COSTA
  Il barbiere di Siviglia, 1946.
  L'elisir d'amore, 1947.
  Cenerentola, 1948.
  Follie per l'Opera, 1948.
  I Pagliacci, 1948.

*FRANCESCO DE ROBERTIS
  Uomini sul fondo (with Bianchi), 1940.
  La nave bianca (with Rossellini), 1942.
  Alfa Tau, 1943.
  Marinai senza stelle, 1943.
  Uomini e cieli, 1943.
  Fantasmi del Mare, 1948.
  La vita semplice, 1945.

*GIUSEPPE DE SANTIS
  Caccia tragica, 1947.
  Riso amaro, 1948.

101

*VITTORIO DE SICA
Rose scarlatte, 1940.
Maddalena zero in condotta, 1940.
Teresa Venerdi, 1941.
Un garibaldino al covento, 1942.
I bambini ci guardano, 1943.
La porta del cielo, 1945.
Sciuscia, 1945.
Ladri di biciclette, 1948.

*RICCARDO FREDA
Tutta la città canta, 1943.
Aquila nera, 1946.
I Miserabili, 1947.
Non canto più 1945.
Guarany, 1948.
Il cavaliere misterioso, 1948.

*ALBERTO LATTUADA
La freccia nel fianco, 1943.
Il bandito, 1946.
Il delitto di Giovanni Episcopo, 1947.
Senza Pietà, 1947.
Il mulino del Po, 1948.

*ROBERTO ROSSELLINI
La nave bianca (with De Robertis, 1942).
Un pilota ritorna, 1942.
I tre aquilotti, (Director Mattoli, 1942).
L'uomo dalla croce, 1943.
Desiderio, 1944.
Roma città aperta, 1944.
Paisa, 1946.

Germania anno zero, 1947.
Amore (1) La Voce Umana, 1947.
(2) Il miracolo, 1948.
La macchina amazzacattivi, 1948.

*MARIO SOLDATI
Due milioni per un sorriso,
(with Borghesio), 1939.
Dora Nelson, 1939.
Tutto per la donna, 1940.
Piccolo mondo antico, 1941.
Tragica notte, 1942.
Malombra, 1942.
Quartieri alti, 1943.
Le miserie di Monsu Travet, 1945.
Eugenia Grandet, 1946.
Daniele Cortis, 1947.
Fuga in Francia, 1949.

*LUCHINO VISCONTI
Ossessione, 1942.
La terra trema, 1948.

*LUIGI ZAMPA
L'attore scomparso, 1941.
Fra Diavolo, 1942.
Signorinette, 1942.
C'è sempre un ma, 1942.
L'abito nero da sposa, 1943.
Un americano in vacanza, 1945.
L'Onerevole Angelina, 1947.
Vivere in pace, 1947.
Anni difficili, 1948.

Appendix II.

CAST AND CREDIT LISTS FOR SOME OF THE MORE IMPORTANT POST-WAR FILMS

AMORE

	LA VOCE UMANA	*IL MIRACOLO*
Producer	Roberto Rossellini	Roberto Rossellini.
Director	Roberto Rossellini	Roberto Rossellini.
Director of Photography	Robert Guillard	Aldo Tonti.
Screen Play	Jean Cocteau (*La Voix Humaine*)	Federico Fellini.
Music	Renzo Rossellini	Renzo Rossellini.
Cast	Anna Magnani	Anna Magnani. Federico Fellini. Villagers of Amalfi and neighbourhood.

ANNI DIFFICILI

Producer	Folco Laudati.
Director	Luigi Zampa.
Director of Photography	Carlo Montuori.
Screen Play	Sergio Amidei and Vitaliano Brancati from a story by Vitaliano Brancati.
Music	Franco Casavola.

CAST:

ALDO PISCITELLO	Umberto Spadaro.
GIOVANNI	Massimo Girotti.
MARIA	Milly Vitale.
ROSINA	Ave Ninchi.
THE MAYOR	Enzo Biliotti.
NONNIN	Ernesto Almirante
RICCARDO	Carletto Sposito.
ELENA	Odette Bedogni.

EUGENIA GRANDET

Produced by	Ferruccio De Martino.
Directed by	Mario Soldati.
Director of Photography	Vaclav Vich.
Screen Play	Aldo De Benedetti and Mario Soldati.
Music by	Renzo Rossellini.

CAST:

Eugenia Grandet	Alida Valli.
Felice Grandet	Gualtiero Tumiati.
Carlo Grandet	Giorgio De Lullo.
Mrs. Grandet	Giuditta Rissone.
Nanon	Pina Gallina.
The Notary Cruchet	Enzo Billotti.
Abbott Cruchet	Lando Sguazzini.
President Cruchet	Cesare Olivieri.
De Grassis, Banker	Giuseppe Verni.
Mrs. De Grassis	Maria Rodi.
Corneiller	Mario Siletti.
Marchioness D'Aubrien	Lina Gennari.
Marquis D' Aubrien	Egisto Olivieri.
Clorinda d'Aubrien	Gabriella Bornura.

FABIOLA

Producer	Attilio Fattori.
Director	Alessandro Blasetti.
Director of Photography	M. Craveri.
Screen Play	M. Chiari, D. Fabbri, C. Zavattini, A. Blasetti, S. Cecchi, A. Fabbri.
Music	Enzo Masetti.

CAST:

Fabiola	Michele Morgan.
Fabio	Michel Simon.
Quadrato	Gino Cervi.
Rhual	Henri Vidal.
Fulvio	Louis Salou.
Sebastiano	Massimo Girotti.
The Proconsul	
Manlio Valerio	Paolo Stoppa.
Luciano	Sergio Tofano.
The Prefect	
Gallo	Carlo Ninchi.

GERMANIA ANNO ZERO !

Producer	Roberto Rossellini.
Director	Roberto Rossellini.
Screen Play	Roberto Rossellini.
Director of Photography	Robert Juillard.
Music	Renzo Rossellini.

CAST:

Edmund Mascke.
Franz Krueger.
Barbara Hintze.

LADRI DI BICICLETTE

Producer	Umberto Scarpelli.
Director	Vittorio De Sica.
Director of Photography	Carlo Montuori.

104

Screen Play	Cesare Zavattini, Oreste Biancoli, Suso d'Amico, Vittorio De Sica, Adolfo Franci, Gerardo Guerrieri.
Music	Alessandro Cicognini.

CAST:

ANTONIO	Lamberto Maggiorani.
BRUNO	Enzo Staiola.
MARIA	Lianella Carell.
THE DUSTMAN	Gino Saltamerenda.
THE OLD MAN	Giulio Chiari.

LA MACCHINA AMMAZZACATTIVI

Producer	Roberto Rossellini.
Director	Roberto Rossellini.
Directors of Photography	Dino Santoni and Edmondo Albertini.
Screen Play	Sergio Amidei and Roberto Rossellini from an idea by Eduardo de Filippo and Fabrizio Sarazani.
Music	Renzo Rossellini.

CAST:

Marylin Buferd (Miss America 1947)
Joe Falletta.
Bill Tubbs.
Helen Tubbs.

———

Giovanni Amato.
Clara Bindi.
Camillo Buonanni.
Giacomo Turia.
Aldo Giuffré.
Aldo Nanni.
Gennaro Pisano.
Gaio Visconti.
and many of the inhabitants of Majori, Amalfi and Atrani.

MIO FIGLIO PROFESSORE

Producer	Clemente Fracassi.
Director	Renato Castellani.
Director of Photography	Carlo Montuori.
Screen Play	R. Castellani, S. Cecchi d'Amico, A. De Benedetti, A. Fabrizi, F. Palmieri.
Music by	Nino Rota.

CAST:

ORAZIO	Aldo Fabrizi.
CONCITA, LISETTE, DIANA	The 3 Nava Sisters.
PROFESSOR GIRALDI	Mario Pisu.
PROFESSOR CARDELLI	Mario Soldati.
ORAZIO JR.	Giorgio De Lullo.

105

LE MISERIE DI MONSU TRAVET

Producer	Dino De Laurentis.
Director	Mario Soldati.
Director of Photography	Massimo Terzano.
Screen Play	A. De Benedetti, T. Pinelli, M. Soldati.
From a Comedy by	Vittorio Bersezio.
Music by	Nino Rota.
Sets by	Luigi Filippone.

CAST:

IGNAZIO TRAVET	Carlo Campanini.
ROSA, his wife	Vera Carmi.
THE COMMENDATORE	Gino Cervi.
DEPARTMENTAL MANAGER	Luigi Pavese.
MARIANIN	Paola Veneroni.
PAOLINO	Enrico Effernelli.
BARBAROTTI	Alberto Sordi.
BRIGIDA	Laura Gore.
GIACHETTA	Domenico Gambino.
CARLUCCIO	Pier Luigi Verando.

L'ONOREVOLE ANGELINA

Producer	Paolo Frascà.
Director	Luigi Zampa.
Director of Photography	Paolo Craveri.
Screen Play	Tellini, D'Amico, Zampa, Magnani.
Music by	Enzo Masetti.

CAST:

ANGELINA	Anna Magnani.
PASQUALE	Nando Bruno.
CARMELA	Ave Ninchi.
CESIRA	Agnese Dubbini.
LUIGI	Ernesto Almirante.
CALLISTO	Armando Migliari.
MR. GARRONE	Mario Donati.
ANNETTA	Maria Grazia Francia.
ROBERT	Vittorio Mottini.
LUIGI FILIPPO	Franco Zeffirelli.

PAISA

Directed by	Roberto Rossellini.
Produced by	Roberto Rossellini.
Screen Play by	Sergio Amidei, Roberto Rossellini, Marcello Pagliero, Federico Fellini.
Director of Photography	Enrico Martelli.
Music by	Renzo Rossellini.

CAST:

Sicilian Episode

AMERICAN SOLDIER	Robert Van Loon.
SICILIAN GIRL	Carmela Sazio.

106

Neapolitan Episode
   NEGRO M.P.   Dats Johnson.
   NEAPOLITAN BOY   Alfonsino.
Roman Episode
   AMERICAN SOLDIER   Gar Moore.
   ROMAN GIRL   Maria Michi.
Florentine Episode
   NURSE   Harriet White.
   PARTISAN   Renzo Avanzo.
Monastery Episode
   CATHOLIC CHAPLAIN   Bill Tubbs.
Romagna Episode
   AMERICAN O.S.S. MAN.   Dale Edmonds.
   PARTISAN   Cigolani.

ROMA CITTA' APERTA (ROME OPEN CITY)

Directed by   Roberto Rossellini.
Produced by   Roberto Rossellini.
Story by   Sergio Amidei.
Screen Play by   Sergio Amidei and Federico Fellini.
Director of Photography   Ubaldo Arata.
Music by   Renzo Rossellini.

CAST:

DON PIETRO   Aldo Fabrizi.
PINA   Anna Magnani.
MANFREDI   Marcello Pagliero.
MARINA   Maria Michi.
BERGMAN   Harry Feist.
INGRID   Giovanna Galletti.
MARCELLO (Pina's child)   Vito Annicchiarico.
LAURETTA   Carla Rovere.
HARTMAN   Van Hulzen.
CHIEF OF POLICE   C. Sindici.
AUSTRIAN DESERTER   Akos Tolnay.

SCIUSCIA (SHOE-SHINE)

Producer   Paolo Tamburella.
Director   Vittorio de Sica.
Director of Photography   Anchise Brizzi.
Screen Play   Sergio Amidei, Adolfo Franci, C. G. Viola,
                      Cesare Zavattini.
Music by   Alessandro Cicognini.

CAST:

GIUSEPPE   Rinaldo Smordoni.
PASQUALE   Franco Interlenghi.
RAFFAELE   Aniello Mele.
ARCANGELI   Bruno Ortensi.
VITTORIO   Pacifico Astrologo.

CIRIELA	Francesco De Nicola.
L'ABRUZZESE	Antonio Carlino.
GIORGIO	Enrico de Silva.
RIGHETTO	Antonio Le Nigre.
SICILIANO	Angelo D'Amico.
STAFFERA	Emilio Cigoli.
AVV. BONAVINO	Giuseppe Spadaro.
COMMISSARIO P.S.	Leo Caravaglia.
IL PANZA	Luigi Saltamerenda.
LA CHIROMANTE	Maria Campi.
LA MAMMA DI GIUSEPPE	Irene Smordoni.
MANNARELLA	Anna Pedoni.

SENZA PIETA

Producer	Clemente Fracassi.
Director	Alberto Lattuada.
Director of Photography	Aldo Tonti.
Screen Play	Federico Fellini, Alberto Lattuada and Tullio Pinella.
Music	Nino Rota.

CAST:

ANGELA	Carla Del Poggio.
JERRY	John Kitzmiller.
PIER LUIGI	Pierre Claudé.
GIACOMO	Folco Lulli.
MARCELLA	Giulietta Masina.
THE SOUTH AMERICAN CAPTAIN	Lando Muzio.

LA TERRA TREMA

Producer	Renato Silvestri.
Director	Luchino Visconti.
Director of Photography	G. R. Aldo.
Screen Play	Luchino Visconti, from the book of the same name by Giovanni Verga.
Music	L. Visconti and Willy Ferrero—pieces from popular Sicilian airs.

CAST:
Sicilian Fishermen and their families.

Index of Film Titles

A

	Page
Abbasso la Miseria	82
Abbasso la Ricchezza	82
Acoiaio	45
Aeroporto del Littorio, L'	38
Aldebaran	45
Alfa Tau	87
Americano in Vacanza, Un	95
Amore	63-67 to 69-95
Amore E Patria	12
Amore mio non Muore, L'	16-23
Angelo e il Diavolo, L'	62
Anita Garibaldi	13
Anni Difficili 46-63-83-85 to	86-95
Antonio Meucoi	26
Apocalisse, L'	74
Aquila Nera	78
Armata, Azzurra, L'	38
Arzigogolo, L'	30
Assedio Dell'Alcazar, L'	47-51
Assisi	38
Assunta Spina	21

B

	Page
Bambini in Citta'	92
Bandito, Il	62-79-82-98
Barbiere di Siviglia, Il	77
Batticuore	97
Beatrice Cenci	32
Bella e la Bestia, La	28
Bengasi	47
Ben Hur	31
Bianchi Pascoli	91
Birth of a Nation	19-48
Black Magic	32
Boomerang	59
Borgia, I	26
Brutus	13-16
Buio Insieme, Al	44

C

	Page
Cabiria	17-18
Caccia al Leopardo	12
Caccia Tragica	62-63-73-80
Cacciatori Sottomarini	92
Caduta di Troia, La	15
Cagliostro	32
Call Northside 777	59
Camicia Nera	45
Cammino Degli Eroi, Il	47
Campane a Martello	46
Cane Riconoscente, Il	11
Cantieri Dell'Adriatico	38
Canzone Dell'Amore, La	35-36
Cappello a tre Punte, Il	46
Catilina	13-15
Cavalcata Ardente, La	30
Cavalieri Della Morte, I	13
Cavaliere Misterioso, Il	74-78
Cena Delle Beffe, La	51
Cenere	26
Cenerentola, La	77
Cesar Birotteau	28
Che Distinta Famiglia	62
Cirano di Bergerac	32
Colpo di Pistola, Un	51
Come Persi la Guerra	77-78
Contessa di Parma, La	45
Convegno Supremo	15
Corona di Ferro, La	98
Corte D'Assise	36
Cortili	92

D

	Page
Daniele Cortis	75-96
Dante e Beatrice	16
Darò un Milione	46-97
Delitto di Giovanni Episcopo, Il	76-77-98
Desiderio	62
Diana L'Affascinatrice	21
Dieci Comandamenti, I	62-74
Don Pietro Caruso	21-24
Dramma di Cristo, Il	90
Due Lettere Anonime	34-62-97
Due Modelle, Le	62

	Page
E	
Earth	34
'1860'	44-97
Elisir D'Amore	77
Enfants du Paradis, Les . .	77
Eroi Della Strada, L' . . .	78
Ettore Fieramosca . . .	45
Eugenia Grandet . .	75-76-96
F	
Fabiola	26-50-75-98
Fanciulla di Amalfi, La . .	21
Fantasmi del Mare, I . . .	87
Fedora	21
Fiaccola sotto il Moggio, La .	15
Figaro e la sua Gran Giornata .	37-97
Figlia del Capitano, La .	34-78-97
Figlia del Corsaro Verde, La .	26
Figlia di Jorio, La . .	15
Figlio di Madam Sans Gene, Il .	23
Finis Terrae	34
Fornarina, La . . .	16-27
Freccia nel Fianco, La . .	62-98
Fuga in Francia . . .	96
Fuoco, Il	25
G	
General Line, The . . .	34
Genoveffa di Brabante . .	74
Germania Anno Zero . 63-65-66-94-95	
Gerusalemme Liberata . . .	26
Giacomo L'Idealista . .	97-98
Gigante delle Dolomiti, Il . .	24
Gioconda, La	15
Giovanna D'Arco . . .	16
Giovanni delle Bande Nere .	13
Giovanni, Episcopo . . .	15
Gioventù Perduta . . .	84
Giulio Cesare	26
Giuseppe Verdi	16
Glass Mountain, The . . .	29
Golden Madonna, The . .	29
Granatiere Roland . . .	15
H	
Hamlet	13
Ho visto Brillare le Stelle . .	26

	Page
I	
In Hoc Signo Vinces . . .	16
Indiana, L'	28
Innocente Casimiro, L' . .	62
Intolerance . . .	19-25-48
Isole della Laguna . . .	91
Isole di Cenere	92
J	
Judith of Bethullia . . .	19
K	
Kif-Tebbi	32
L	
Ladri di Biciclette . 12-36-63-79-80	
Lady of the Camellias . . 16-23-25	
Land of Mussolini's Birth . .	90
Last Days of Pompeii, The . 16-17-32	
Leggenda di Faust, La . .	30
Lezione in Geometria, Una .	92
Littoria e Mussolinia di Sardegna	38
London Day by Day . . .	39
Lorenzino DeMedici . . .	46
Lucia di Lammermoor . .	77
Luciano Serra Pilota . . .	51
Lucrezia Borgia . . . 13-15	
M	
Ma Non E Una Cosa Seria .	97
Macchina Ammazzacattivi, La	
	63-69-70-95
Maciste All'Inferno . .	24
Maciste Contro la Morte . .	24
Maciste Contro lo Sceicco . .	24
Maciste Nella Gabbia dei Leoni	24
Madame Sans Gene . . 23-25	
Malia 21-62	
Malombra	96
Marcantonio e Cleopatra . .	26
Marinai Senza Stelle . . 86-87	
Medico per Forza . . .	36
Messalina	26
Mio Figlio Professore . . 44-51-97	
Miracle of the Bells, The . .	75
Miracolo, Il . . . 68-69-99	
Miserabili, I 73-78	
Miserie di Monsu Travet, Le 44-75-96	
Molti Sogni per le Strade . 34-97	
Mondo Vuole Cosi, Il . .	62

110

		Page
N		
Naked City, The	. . .	59
Nanook	. . . .	85
Nave Bianca, La	. . .	87-94
Nave, La	. . . .	15
Nine Men	. . .	47
Notte Romantica, Una	. .	28
Nuccia la Pecoraia	. . .	12

		Page
O		
O la Borsa O la Vita	. . .	44
Odette	. . . .	21
Onorevole Angelina, L'	.	63-83-85-96
Ora Muoio Lieta	. .	12
Oro Nero	. . . .	27
Ossessione	. .	53 to 56-99
Ostrega Che Sbrego	. . .	37

P		
Paestum	. . .	38
Paisà	63 to 65-74-95-99	
Pallio	. . . .	37
Pantera di Neve, La	. .	28
Paradiso	. . .	44
Perdono del Nonno, Il	. .	12
Piacere, Il	. . .	15
Piccolo Mondo Antico	.	52-96-97
Pilota Ritorna, Un	. .	51-94
Pinocchio	. . .	15
Pirati della Malesia, I	.	27
Porta del Cielo, La	. .	79
Prince of Foxes, The	.	31-32-50
Principessa Tarakanova, La	.	96
Processo Clemenceau, Il	.	21
Processo delle Zitelle, Il	.	62
Promessi Sposi, I	. .	16

Q		
Quartetto Pazzo	. . .	62-82
Quattro Passi fra le Nuvore		37-51-96
Quo Vadis?	.	16-17-26-29-30-48

R		
Ratto delle Sabine, Il	. .	62
Re Burlone	. . .	46
Rendenzione di Faust, La	.	77
Resurrectio	. . .	36
Retaggio di Odio	. .	25
Rigoletto	. . .	77
Ritorno al Nido	. . .	62

		Page
Roma Città Aperta	34-57 to 62-78-79-95	
Romantica Avventura, Una	.	97
Romantici di Venezia, I	.	91
Romanticismo	. . .	16
Romanzo di un Giovane Povero, Il		15
Romola	. . .	30-31
Rosa di Tebe	. . .	15-21
Rosa, La	. . .	28
Rose Rouge, La	. . .	15
Rotaie	. . .	34-97
Rubacuori	. . .	36

S		
Sacco di Roma, Il	. . .	26
Sangue Blu	. . .	21
Sardanapalo	. .	13
Sbaglio di Essere Vivo, Lo	.	62
Scadenza Giorni Trenta	.	62
Scala di Seta, La	. .	28
Schiavo di Cartagine	. .	13
Scipione L'Africano	.	40-48
Sciuscia	.	36-37-62-78-79
Second Mrs. Tanqueray, The	.	22
Seconda B	. . .	44
Seconda Moglie, La	. .	22
Sentinelle di Bronzo	. .	46
Senza Pietà	.	74-84-98
Shoulder Arms	. . .	77
Siegfried	. . .	15
Signor Max, Il	. .	97
Signora delle Camelie, La	.	21-77
Sole	. .	33-34-35
Sole Sorge Ancora, Il	.	73-80
Sotto Il Sole di Roma	.	51-63
Sotto la Croce del sud	. .	46
Sperduti nel Buio	. .	25
Squadrone Bianco, Lo	.	46
Storia di Manon Lescaut, La	.	22
Storia di Un Pierrot, La	.	24-25
Stromboli	.	63-70-72
Suo Bambino, Il	. .	38
Suo Destino, Il	. . .	26
Sulla via di Damasco	. .	90

T		
Tavola dei Poveri, La	. .	44
Teodora	. .	26-29
Terra Madre	. .	36
Terra Trema, La	. .	13-84
Terremotod di Messina, Il	.	12

	Page
Tigre Reale, La	22
Tombolo	84
Tonnara	92
Topi Grigi	25
Tosca	21
Tre Aquilotti, Il . . .	50

U

Ultimi Giorni di Pompei, Gli	
	16-26-50-75
Ultimo dei Frontignac, L' . .	15
Un Giorno Nella Vita . .	62-98
Uomini Che Mascalzoni, Gli .	37-97
Uomini e Cieli . . .	87
Uomini sul Fondo . . .	87
Uomo Più Allegro di Vienna, L'	30

V

	Page
Vecchia Guardia . . .	45
Vecchia Signora, La . . .	36
Vele Ammainate . . .	36
Ventre della Città, Il . . .	38
Vita Semplice, La . . .	87-88
Vivere in Pace	37-46-62-74-81-83-85-96
Voce Umana, La . . .	67-68
Vulcano	19

W

White Sister, The . . .	30-31

Z

Zara	38

Index of Names

A

Aldo, G. R. . . . 85
Alessandrini, Goffredo . . 44-51
Alliata, Prince . . . 91-92
Almirante, Luigi . . . 46
Ambrosio, Arturo . . 11-15-29
Amidei, Sergio . . . 57
A.N.P.I. 78
Arata, Ubaldo . . . 34-51-58
Assicurazioni Nazionali . . 43
Associazione Nazionale
    Combattenti 43

B

Banca, Del Lavoro . . . 40
Barattolo, Giuseppe . . . 36
Bassoli, Carlo . . . 47-51
Bava, Mario . . . 92
Belmonte, Michela . . . 50
Bencivenga, Edoardo. . . 13
Benetti, Adriana . . . 51
Bergman, Ingrid . . 70-71-72
Bertini, Francesca 15-20-21-23-24-25-36
Blasetti, Alessandro . 33-34-36-37-38-
    44-45-46-51-75-97-99
Bonnard, Mario . 16-20-23-29
Borelli, Lyda . 16-20-22-23-25
Borghesio, Carlo . . . 78
Bragaglia, Anton Giulio . . 36
Bragag'ia, Carlo L. . . . 44
Brignone, Guido . 24-36-44-46
Bruno, Nando . . . 83
Bugnano, Marchese di . . 14

C

Caesar . . 13-21-23-36-38
Calamai, Clara . . . 51-54
Camerini, Mario 24-32-34-37-46-95-96
Campanini, Carlo . . 75-81
Campogalliani . . . 24
Capozzi, Alberto . . 15-16-20
Carmi, Vera . . . 65
Carminati Tullio . . . 29
Caserini . . . 13-15-23

Cassa, Infortuni . . . 43
Castellani, Renato . . 44-51
Cavalieri, Lina . . 20-22-29
Cecchi, Emilio . . . 38
Centro, Sperimentale . . 48-49
Cervi, Gino . . 46-51-76
Chiarini, Luigi . . . 48-49
Chili 74
Cicognini, Alessandro. . . 46
Cinecitta'. . . . 49-50
Cines . . 13-15-21-35-38
Collo, Alberto . . . 25
Cortese, Valentina . . . 51
Cortometraggi . . . 91
Costa, Mario . . . 24-77
Cretinetti 12

D

D'Angelo, Salvo . . . 73-83
D'Annunzio, Gabriele 14-15-17-18-76
De Filippo, Eduardo . 21-46-69
De Filippo, Peppino . . 46
De Landa, Juan . . . 54
De Liguoro, Rina . . 22-29
Del Poggio, Carla . . 82-84
Denis, Maria . . . 44-45
De Robertis, Francesco 86 to 88-94
De Santis, Giuseppe . . 64-78
De Sica, Vittorio . 36-37-46-78 to 80
Duse, Eleonora . . . 26-62

E

Emmer, Luciano . . 89 to 91
E.N.A.I.P.E. . . . 41
E.N.I.C. 42

F

Fabrizi, Aldo . 59-81-82-84-95
Fassini, Barone Alberto . . 14
Feist, Harry . . . 59
Ferida, Luisa . . . 51-52
Fosco, Piero . . 15-17-25
Fracchia, Umberto . . 28
Frateili, Arnaldo . . . 28

G

Gallone, Carmine   .   29-30-32-48-77
Genina, Augusto   .   21-29-47-51
Germi, Pietro 84
Ghione, Emilio .   .   . 20-23-25-30
Giachetti, Fosco   .   .   . 47-48
Girotti, Massimo   .   . 54-75-84
Gras, Enrico .   .   . 89 to 91
Guazzoni, Enrico   .   . 16-26-46-74
Gys, Leda   25

H

Hall-Davis, Lilian   .   .   . 29
Hesperia 22-23-25

J

Jacobini, Maria .   .   16-29-32
Jacoby, Georg .   .   . 29
Jannings, Emil .   .   . 29

K

King, Henry   .   .   . 30
Kitzmiller, John   .   .   . 84
Korda, Maria   .   .   . 30-32

L

Lattuada, Alberto 64-76-77-82-84-97-98
Lombardo, Goffredo .   .   . 13
Lombardo, Gustavo .   .   . 13
L.U.C.E. 39-42
Lulli, Folco   .   .   . 84-97
Lux Film 74-96

M

Macario   77
Maciste   .   .   . 18-20-23-24
Magnani, Anna   21-23-44-58-59-67 to
69-82-83-95-97
Marcuzzi, Elio 54
Menichelli, Pina   .   .   . 22
Michi, Maria   .   . 57-58-64-95
Minculpop   .   .   . 40
Monicelli, Mario   .   . 78
Montuori, Carlo   .   .   . 12
Moore, Gar   .   .   . 64-74
Mussolini, Benito   .   . 21
Mussolini, Vittorio   .   . 50-51

N

Nazzari, Amedeo   .   . 51-52-82

Negroni, Baldassare .   .   . 25-32
Novelli, Amleto   .   . 15-21-26

O

Omegma, Rodolfo .   .   . 12
Oxilia, Nino   .   .   . 16

P

Pacelli, Marchese Ernesto .   . 13
Pagano, Bartolomeo .   . 18-23
Palermi, Amleto   .   . 32-36
Panaria 91-92
Pasquali, Ernesto   .   . 11-16
Pastrone, Giovanni   .   . 17
Petrolini, Ettore   .   .   . 36
Picasso, Lamberto   .   . 28
Pirandello, Luigi   .   . 28-45
Pittaluga, Stefano   . 32-35-38
Pizzetti, Ildebrando   .   . 19-48
Polidor 12-15
Ponti, Carlo   .   .   . 91

R

Rabagliati, Alberto   .   .   . 30
Rabinovich   .   .   . 30
Righelli, Gennaro   . 35-38-44-82
Risi, Dino   .   .   . 92
Robinet 12
Rossellini, Renzo   .   . 61-69
Rossellini, Roberto   34-50-51-57 to 72-
82-94-95
Ruttman 45

S

San Servolo, Myria di   .   . 50
Scotese, G. M. .   .   . 74
Sernas, Jaques .   .   . 84
Sinisgalli, Leonardo   .   . 92
Soldati, Mario .   37-44-51-75-76-96-97
Spadaro, Umberto   .   .   . 85
Stafford, John .   .   . 29
Steno   78
Sutro, John   .   .   . 29

T

Tarlarini, Mary Cleo .   . 15-16-20
Tespi   28
Tiber   .   .   . 13-21-23
Tontolini 12
Tubbs, Bill   .   .   . 64

U

Unione Cinematografica Italiana.   28
Universalia   .   26-74-75-84-85

V

Valenti, Osvaldo   .   .   46-51-52
Valli, Alida   .   .   .   75
Vergano, Aldo 33-80
Visconti, Luchino   .   . 53-54-84-85
Vitiello, Elena   20

W

White, Harriet 64-74

Z

Za La Mort   .   .   .   24
Zampa, Luigi   .   . 81-83-85-95-96
Zeglio   74

115

The Arno Press Cinema Program

THE LITERATURE OF CINEMA

Series I & II

American Academy of Political and Social Science. **The Motion Picture in Its Economic and Social Aspects,** edited by Clyde L. King. **The Motion Picture Industry,** edited by Gordon S. Watkins. *The Annals,* November, 1926/1927.

Agate, James. **Around Cinemas.** 1946.

Agate, James. **Around Cinemas.** (Second Series). 1948.

Balcon, Michael, Ernest Lindgren, Forsyth Hardy and Roger Manvell. **Twenty Years of British Film, 1925-1945.** 1947.

Bardèche, Maurice and Robert Brasillach. **The History of Motion Pictures,** edited by Iris Barry. 1938.

Benoit-Levy, Jean. **The Art of the Motion Picture.** 1946.

Blumer, Herbert. **Movies and Conduct.** 1933.

Blumer, Herbert and Philip M. Hauser. **Movies, Delinquency, and Crime.** 1933.

Buckle, Gerard Fort. **The Mind and the Film.** 1926.

Carter, Huntly. **The New Spirit in the Cinema.** 1930.

Carter, Huntly. **The New Spirit in the Russian Theatre, 1917-1928.** 1929.

Carter, Huntly. **The New Theatre and Cinema of Soviet Russia.** 1924.

Charters, W. W. **Motion Pictures and Youth.** 1933.

Cinema Commission of Inquiry. **The Cinema: Its Present Position and Future Possibilities.** 1917.

Dale, Edgar. **The Content of Motion Pictures.** 1935.

Dale, Edgar. **How to Appreciate Motion Pictures.** 1937.

Dale, Edgar. **Children's Attendance at Motion Pictures.** Dysinger, Wendell S. and Christian A. Ruckmick. **The Emotional Responses of Children to the Motion Picture Situation.** 1935.

Dale, Edgar, Fannie W. Dunn, Charles F. Hoban, Jr., and Etta Schneider. **Motion Pictures in Education: A Summary of the Literature.** 1938.

Davy, Charles. **Footnotes to the Film.** 1938.

Dickinson, Thorold and Catherine De la Roche. **Soviet Cinema.** 1948.

Dickson, W. K. L., and Antonia Dickson. **History of the Kinetograph, Kinetoscope and Kinetophonograph.** 1895.

Forman, Henry James. **Our Movie Made Children.** 1935.

Freeburg, Victor Oscar. **The Art of Photoplay Making.** 1918.

Freeburg, Victor Oscar. **Pictorial Beauty on the Screen.** 1923.

Hall, Hal, editor. **Cinematographic Annual,** 2 vols. 1930/1931.

Hampton, Benjamin B. **A History of the Movies.** 1931.

Hardy, Forsyth. **Scandinavian Film.** 1952.

Hepworth, Cecil M. **Animated Photography: The A B C of the Cinematograph.** 1900.

Hoban, Charles F., Jr., and Edward B. Van Ormer. **Instructional Film Research 1918-1950.** 1950.

Holaday, Perry W. and George D. Stoddard. **Getting Ideas from the Movies.** 1933.

Hopwood, Henry V. **Living Pictures.** 1899.

Hulfish, David S. **Motion-Picture Work.** 1915.

Hunter, William. **Scrutiny of Cinema.** 1932.

Huntley, John. **British Film Music.** 1948.

Irwin, Will. **The House That Shadows Built.** 1928.

Jarratt, Vernon. **The Italian Cinema.** 1951.

Jenkins, C. Francis. **Animated Pictures.** 1898.

Lang, Edith and George West. **Musical Accompaniment of Moving Pictures.** 1920.

L'Art Cinematographique, Nos. 1-8. 1926-1931.

London, Kurt. **Film Music.** 1936.

Lutz, E [dwin] G [eorge]. **The Motion-Picture Cameraman.** 1927.

Manvell, Roger. **Experiment in the Film.** 1949.

Marey, Etienne Jules. **Movement.** 1895.

Martin, Olga J. **Hollywood's Movie Commandments.** 1937.

Mayer, J. P. **Sociology of Film: Studies and Documents.** 1946. New Introduction by J. P. Mayer.

Münsterberg, Hugo. **The Photoplay: A Psychological Study.** 1916.

Nicoll, Allardyce. **Film and Theatre.** 1936.

Noble, Peter. **The Negro in Films.** 1949.

Peters, Charles C. **Motion Pictures and Standards of Morality.** 1933.

Peterson, Ruth C. and L. L. Thurstone. **Motion Pictures and the Social Attitudes of Children.** Shuttleworth, Frank K. and Mark A. May. **The Social Conduct and Attitudes of Movie Fans.** 1933.

Phillips, Henry Albert. **The Photodrama.** 1914.

Photoplay Research Society. **Opportunities in the Motion Picture Industry.** 1922.

Rapée, Erno. **Encyclopaedia of Music for Pictures.** 1925.

Rapée, Erno. **Motion Picture Moods for Pianists and Organists.** 1924.

Renshaw, Samuel, Vernon L. Miller and Dorothy P. Marquis. **Children's Sleep.** 1933.

Rosten, Leo C. **Hollywood: The Movie Colony, The Movie Makers.** 1941.

Sadoul, Georges. **French Film.** 1953.

Screen Monographs I, 1923-1937. 1970.

Screen Monographs II, 1915-1930. 1970.

Sinclair, Upton. **Upton Sinclair Presents William Fox.** 1933.

Talbot, Frederick A. **Moving Pictures.** 1912.

Thorp, Margaret Farrand. **America at the Movies.** 1939.

Wollenberg, H. H. **Fifty Years of German Film.** 1948.

RELATED BOOKS AND PERIODICALS

Allister, Ray. **Friese-Greene: Close-Up of an Inventor.** 1948.

Art in Cinema: A Symposium of the Avant-Garde Film, edited by Frank Stauffacher. 1947.

The Art of Cinema: Selected Essays. New Foreword by George Amberg. 1971.

Balázs, Béla. **Theory of the Film.** 1952.

Barry, Iris. **Let's Go to the Movies.** 1926.

de Beauvoir, Simone. **Brigitte Bardot and the Lolita Syndrome.** 1960.

Carrick, Edward. **Art and Design in the British Film.** 1948.

Close Up. Vols. 1-10, 1927-1933 (all published).

Cogley, John. **Report on Blacklisting. Part I: The Movies.** 1956.

Eisenstein, S. M. **Que Viva Mexico!** 1951.

Experimental Cinema. 1930-1934 (all published).

Feldman, Joseph and Harry. **Dynamics of the Film.** 1952.

Film Daily Yearbook of Motion Pictures. Microfilm, 18 reels, 35 mm. 1918-1969.

Film Daily Yearbook of Motion Pictures. 1970.

Film Daily Yearbook of Motion Pictures. (Wid's Year Book). 3 vols., 1918-1922.

The Film Index: A Bibliography. Vol. I: The Film as Art. 1941.

Film Society Programmes. 1925-1939 (all published).

Films: A Quarterly of Discussion and Analysis. Nos. 1-4, 1939-1940 (all published).

Flaherty, Frances Hubbard. **The Odyssey of a Film-Maker: Robert Flaherty's Story.** 1960.

General Bibliography of Motion Pictures, edited by Carl Vincent, Riccardo Redi, and Franco Venturini. 1953.

Hendricks, Gordon. **Origins of the American Film.** 1961-1966. New Introduction by Gordon Hendricks.

Hound and Horn: Essays on Cinema, 1928-1934. 1971.

Huff, Theodore. **Charlie Chaplin.** 1951.

Kahn, Gordon. **Hollywood on Trial.** 1948.

New York Times Film Reviews, 1913-1968. 1970.

Noble, Peter. **Hollywood Scapegoat: The Biography of Erich von Stroheim.** 1950.

Robson, E. W. and M. M. **The Film Answers Back.** 1939.

Weinberg, Herman G., editor. **Greed.** 1971.

Wollenberg, H. H. **Anatomy of the Film.** 1947.

Wright, Basil. **The Use of the Film.** 1948.